WITHDRAWN FROM
THE LIBRARY

UNIVERSITY OF
WINCHESTER

The inspiration for *Slave to Fashion* came to me in a dream.
The faces and hands of women, children and men reached
out to me, calling, smiling, asking for solidarity, not charity,
and for me to witness and tell their story. (It was not a
nightmare; nightmares leave you trying to forget. In this
dream I wanted to remember the feelings and the
colours, and to reconnect with the people in it.)

They are us and we are them...

Thank you to all the supporters and contributors who
helped to make *Slave to Fashion* happen, and to people
on the team who remain as passionate as I am about
transforming the fashion industry and business world:
Matt Morgan, Miki Alcalde, Liz Wilkinson, Wendy Chapman.
Thanks also to all the photographers who have allowed
us to use their photos free of charge.

Safia Minney

New Internationalist

KA 0431883 8

IN SUPPLY CHAINS WORLDWIDE

21 MI

168 MI

$150 BI

LLION
LLION
LLION

People are victims of forced labour

Children still in child labour

Illicit profits generated annually

UNIVERSITY OF WINCHESTER
LIBRARY

Published in 2017 by:
New Internationalist Publications Ltd
The Old Music Hall
106-108 Cowley Road
Oxford OX4 1JE

newint.org

Author
Safia Minney
www.safiaminney.com

Design & Art Direction
Matt Morgan
www.factstudio.co.uk

Photography & Film
Miki Alcalde
www.mikialcaldemedia.com

Research & Editorial
Elizabeth Wilkinson
@ethicaledit

Editorial
Wendy Chapman

Editor
Jo Lateu New Internationalist

Design & Production
Ian Nixon New Internationalist

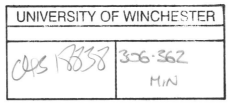

UNIVERSITY OF WINCHESTER

CAS 18838   306·362
              MIN

Names of garment workers have been changed to protect their identity.

The right of Safia Minney to be identified as the author of this work has been asserted in accordance with the Copyright, Design and Patents Act 1998.

All photographs © individual photographers as credited.

All rights reserved. No part of this book may be reproduced, stored in retrieval system or transmitted, in any form or by any means, electronic, electrostatic, magnetic tape, mechanical, photocopying, recording or otherwise, without prior permission in writing of the Publisher.

© Safia Minney 2017

While every effort has been taken to ensure accuracy, the Publisher cannot be held responsible for errors or omissions. No responsibility for loss occasioned to any person acting or refraining from action as a result of material in this publication can be accepted by the Publisher.

Printed in Italy by Graphicom.

British Library Cataloguing-in-Publication Data

A catalogue record for this book is available from the British Library.

Library of Congress Cataloging-in-Publication Data

A catalog record for this book is available from the Library of Congress.

MIX
Paper from
responsible sources
FSC® C013123

ISBN paperback: 978-1-78026-398-4
ISBN ebook: 978-1-78026-399-1

1

The Modern Slavery Act

What is it? How are governments, human rights organizations and trade unions giving slaves a voice?
And what can industry bodies do to improve their practices?

Contents

We are the change!

I started to think about modern slavery many years ago, when I saw an eight-year-old boy lying sick on the dirty floor of a slum workshop. Having a son the same age, I trembled with the anger and injustice of it, and I never forgot him.

As founder and CEO of People Tree, the Fair Trade company I set up in Japan 25 years ago, I was able to make sure that at least some garment workers in Bangladesh and India could escape the horrors which are widespread in our fast-fashion profit-driven clothing industry. I developed the first Fair Trade supply chains and helped to create social and organic standards to improve the lives of over 5,000 economically marginalized people in the developing world.

Working on this book has given me the chance to take stock of what we have achieved as a Fair Trade and social justice movement, the extent to which we have helped to shape current business practice and thinking, and what more needs to be done to finally end modern slavery. There have been some significant gains recently: Britain's Modern Slavery Act, which came into force in 2015, and which you can read more about in Chapter 1, was inspired by the California Transparency in Supply Chains Act and by three decades of campaigning for Fair Trade, social justice and ethical consumption. It is a good start, and as a result

of the Act, companies must now publish details of their supply chains, forcing them to be more aware of what is happening further down the production process and beyond the so-called 'first tier' suppliers – with whom brands have direct contact, but who often subcontract work to other factories or individuals. It is much harder now for brand owners and boards of directors to turn a blind eye to the conditions in which their clothes are made.

Despite the gains, there is still much to be done. Civil-society groups and consumers need to evolve their role as they continue to speak up for modern slaves and challenge brands' business practices. The rapid advance of social media and access to digital technology across much of the globe can help us, and the workers themselves, raise awareness, and in Chapter 4 we meet innovative businesses that are doing just that.

Whether or not we are members or supporters of campaign groups fighting for an end to modern slavery (and if you're not, see our Resources list on page 158 for how to get involved!), we are all consumers. This means that all of us have the power to demand change from the companies we buy from. We can demand that they guarantee that their products are made sustainably and free of slavery. We can accept that paying a little more for the goods we buy

is the right thing to do if it helps ensure garment workers are paid a living wage.

We are all consumers – but many of us are also workers. So we can learn from best practice in the companies that are leading the way in sustainable, fair business. We can help bring our own companies up to speed. Those of us working for government or in financial institutions can set new measures for prosperity, question our dysfunctional capitalist system and strive for a fairer world that puts people and planet ahead of profit. If we are working in the media, we can move towards constructive journalism and expose what is really happening in our world.

NGOs and campaigning groups already have a vision for change: they know that innovation, positivity and collaboration with brands, governments and trade unions is the key to liberating people caught in modern slavery and to changing the business and environment in which it operates.

So what can we, as individuals and consumers, campaigners and workers, do to help make this vision a reality? We need to lean in and learn. We need to show humility, vision and drive and lend our voice and power to help eradicate slavery. We need to buy more consciously and support the organizations and companies pushing for change. And we need

Miki Alcalde

to demand that our governments create a central, open list of companies that are legally required to report on their supply chains and ensure that they comply.

Slave to Fashion provides the background on the various areas – from law and technology to business, social enterprise, campaigning and media – which can drive change. It also offers a toolkit so that you can get informed and get involved (see Chapter 5).

This book is a snapshot of a particular moment in time. Things are changing quickly and we are witnessing exciting developments that could lead to a whole new economic approach that values people's labour, livelihoods and community and our natural resources, that acknowledges indigenous wisdom and culture and that delivers democracy and gender equality. A new, enlightened business model could transform the world as we know it. This is not just a question of eradicating modern slavery; it is a question of transforming a profit-driven capitalist world into a sustainable model that ensures the survival of humanity and of our planet.

And the wonderful thing is, we all have a creative and leadership role to play.

Safia worked for over 20 years with organic cotton farmers, artisans and tailors to bring pioneering Fair Trade, social development and environmental protection throughout the People Tree supply chain.

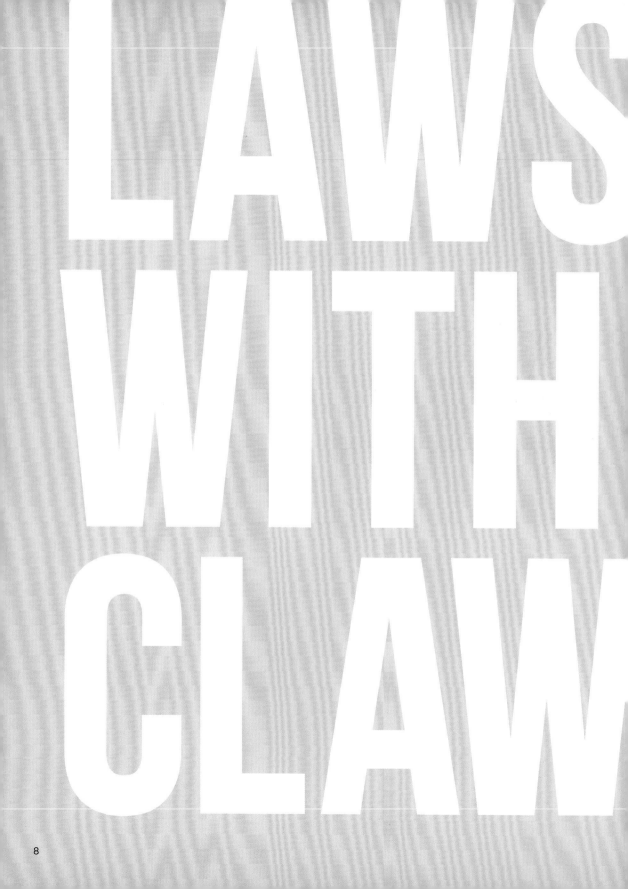

LAWS
WITH
CLAW

WHAT IS MODERN SLAVERY?

Although it is illegal, there are more people trapped in slavery today than ever before. Millions of vulnerable men, women and children are enslaved through human trafficking and forced labour.

Bangle-making near Delhi, India, where children as young as four work to supplement their family income.

There are many reasons why millions are trapped in modern slavery. From political decisions and population growth to a lack of choice and opportunity for the poor; from the undermining and theft of the natural environment upon which many of the world's poorest people depend for their livelihoods – including access to the sea, forests and grazing lands – to urban-centric development policy: rural communities in the Majority World are left jobless, hungry, struggling in poverty and vulnerable to exploitation and forms of modern slavery.

Where laws exist they are not implemented, and corruption may run in the police force and government itself. Slavery exists in an enormous, thriving black economy; we consumers have never before 'enjoyed' such economic benefit from the slave trade as we do today. Criminal gangs line their pockets with the profits from human trafficking and consumers get cheaper clothes, foods and electronics. Thanks to a dysfunctional capitalist system, global corporations, shareholders, banks and investors, and financial institutions make handsome profits and huge dividends – in many cases off the backs of slaves. Modern slavery is an umbrella term used to describe its various forms, including:

Child Labour – Children are in slavery as domestic workers, or used as forced labour in the supply chains of clothing, jewellery and agricultural products such as cotton, cocoa and fisheries. They are trafficked for labour and for sexual exploitation, or as child soldiers. In Chapter 3 we meet proud but tired 14- and 15-year-olds who toil for 60 hours a week in garment factories and whose meagre salary is used to support their parents and siblings.

Human Trafficking – This is the transport or trade of children and adults from one area to another and into conditions of slavery. It is often done through deceptive recruitment and coercion. The fact that the victim's family is often tricked into agreeing to the 'deal' makes them feel complicit in the crime and unwilling to report it or to prosecute the traffickers. On page 62 you will read about Prakash and his victims. Prakash is building himself a grand house with the profits made from trading young women into Kolkata, Delhi and Mumbai.

Forced and Excessive Labour – This is when people are forced to work through threats or intimidation. People often find themselves trapped, sometimes far from home. In Chapter 3 we will meet garment workers who are forced to work long hours without a break or even a day off. Often they work without contracts. Their managers are abusive and they are afraid of losing their job if they attempt to protect themselves or their rights.

Bonded Labour – People become bonded labourers after falling into debt and being forced to work for free in an attempt to repay it. Many will never pay off their loans and debt can be passed down to the next generation. On page 65 we meet Aloysius in Tirupur, who helps adolescent girls free themselves from the Sumangali scheme, a form of bonded labour. Under the Sumangali scheme, young girls are trapped in cotton mills and garment factories for three years and are paid a fraction of the minimum wage.

The UK Modern Slavery Act

The Modern Slavery Act (nin.tl/MSlavery-Act) came into force in October 2015. Designed to tackle slavery and trafficking, it was a game-changer, because it requires any commercial company with a global turnover of at least £36 million ($45 million) and that trades within the UK to produce an annual slavery and human-trafficking statement. The statement must contain details of the steps that the company has taken in the financial year to identify and eradicate modern slavery from both its own business and its supply chain or, if this is the case, to state that no steps have been taken. The Act galvanizes initiatives to promote better business practice and transparency in supply chains and is shaping a new social dialogue as companies, trade unions, NGOs and governments find ways to tackle slavery. Only a collaborative approach such as this will deliver transparency, decent wages for all workers, gender equality, and policies that have social justice at their heart.

As it stands, the Act requires companies to prepare and publish their statement about slavery in their supply chain. To date, the Act does not stipulate that they have to take action to eradicate slavery. However, the UK government envisages that commercial pressure will be brought to bear on those companies that fail to take action.

The new law will make transparent what a particular company is or is not doing, thus enabling members of the public, employees, consumers and investors to make informed decisions about whom to do business with. Statements (and failures to produce them) are likely to attract the attention of civil society and sections of the media that report on social justice and human rights issues. The consequences of failing to take the issue seriously, in terms of reputational damage and competitive disadvantage, could be significant.

The power to make change

Consumers and campaigning groups have a unique opportunity to accelerate the implementation of the Modern Slavery Act. We can draw on 30 years of campaigns for Fair Trade, ethical business, social justice, corporate accountability and environmentalism to put pressure on companies for slave-free products. Together with pioneering businesses and enlightened policymakers, we have the power to change how products are made, to protect workers and farmers, and to reward companies for good practice by buying their products.

Companies that work to manage their supply chains and the risks of slavery, together with better government policy, can help to eradicate slavery and tackle the root causes of power imbalances while putting the real social and environmental costs into the price of products. They can also set the agenda for better business so that others in their sector can follow.

But this will only happen through sustained consumer pressure and awareness. So what are we waiting for? Let's tell our companies and our politicians what we want, and reward companies that show openness, integrity and true courage in promoting a type of business that promotes human rights and sets standards for best practice.

PART 6
TRANSPARENCY IN SUPPLY CHAINS ETC

54 Transparency in supply chains etc

(1) A commercial organisation within subsection (2) must prepare a slavery and human trafficking statement for each financial year of the organisation.

(2) A commercial organisation is within this subsection if it—

(a) supplies goods or services, and

(b) has a total turnover of not less than an amount prescribed by regulations made by the Secretary of State.

(3) For the purposes of subsection (2)(b), an organisation's total turnover is to be determined in accordance with regulations made by the Secretary of State.

(4) A slavery and human trafficking statement for a financial year is—

(a) a statement of the steps the organisation has taken during the financial year to ensure that slavery and human trafficking is not taking place—

(i) in any of its supply chains, and

(ii) in any part of its own business, or

(b) a statement that the organisation has taken no such steps.

(5) An organisation's slavery and human trafficking statement may include information about—

(a) the organisation's structure, its business and its supply chains;

(b) its policies in relation to slavery and human trafficking;

(c) its due diligence processes in relation to slavery and human trafficking in its business and supply chains;

(d) the parts of its business and supply chains where there is a risk of slavery and human trafficking taking place, and the steps it has taken to assess and manage that risk;

(e) its effectiveness in ensuring that slavery and human trafficking is not taking place in its business or supply chains, measured against such performance indicators as it considers appropriate;

(f) the training about slavery and human trafficking available to its staff.

(6) A slavery and human trafficking statement—

(a) if the organisation is a body corporate other than a limited liability partnership, must be approved by the board of directors (or equivalent management body) and signed by a director (or equivalent);

(b) if the organisation is a limited liability partnership, must be approved by the members and signed by a designated member;

(c) if the organisation is a limited partnership registered under the Limited Partnerships Act 1907, must be signed by a general partner;

(d) if the organisation is any other kind of partnership, must be signed by a partner.

(7) If the organisation has a website, it must—

(a) publish the slavery and human trafficking statement on that website, and

(b) include a link to the slavery and human trafficking statement in a prominent place on that website's homepage.

(8) If the organisation does not have a website, it must provide a copy of the slavery and human trafficking statement to anyone who makes a written request for one, and must do so before the end of the period of 30 days beginning with the day on which the request is received.

(9) The Secretary of State—

(a) may issue guidance about the duties imposed on commercial organisations by this section;

(b) must publish any such guidance in a way the Secretary of State considers appropriate.

(10) The guidance may in particular include further provision about the kind of information which may be included in a slavery and human trafficking statement.

(11) The duties imposed on commercial organisations by this section are enforceable by the Secretary of State bringing civil proceedings in the High Court for an injunction or, in Scotland, for specific performance of a statutory duty under section 45 of the Court of Session Act 1988.

(12) For the purposes of this section—

"commercial organisation" means—

(a) a body corporate (wherever incorporated) which carries on a business, or part of a business, in any part of the United Kingdom, or

(b) a partnership (wherever formed) which carries on a business, or part of a business, in any part of the United Kingdom, and for this purpose "business" includes a trade or profession;

"partnership" means—

(a) a partnership within the Partnership Act 1890,

(b) a limited partnership registered under the Limited Partnerships Act 1907, or

(c) a firm, or an entity of a similar character, formed under the law of a country outside the United Kingdom;

"slavery and human trafficking" means—

(a) conduct which constitutes an offence under any of the following—

Setting industry standards

Sam Maher is the co-ordinator on worker safety at the international office of the Clean Clothes Campaign (CCC), which engages consumers in solidarity with garment workers to improve their working conditions. The last time we met up was at a protest outside Benetton's flagship store in London's Oxford Circus in April 2014, when CCC was pushing the brand to pay compensation to the families of garment workers who were killed in the collapse of the Rana Plaza building in Dhaka, Bangladesh, in April 2013. I caught up with Sam to discuss what has changed since the tragedy.

How does CCC work?

We educate and mobilize citizens and consumers, lobby companies and governments, and offer direct solidarity support to workers. We are a global network of about 200 trade unions and NGOs from producing and consuming countries, which brings together

The aftermath of the Rana Plaza factory collapse in Bangladesh, April 2013.

rijans under a CC licence

two ends of the global garment supply chain.

CCC was instrumental in creating the Accord on Fire and Building Safety in Bangladesh, the legally binding agreement between global brands, retailers and trade unions designed to hold

companies accountable for worker safety and compensation. How did you do this?

The Rana Plaza story starts eight years earlier, with the collapse of the Spectrum garment factory in Bangladesh. Spectrum supplied clothes to Inditex/Zara, and in 2005 illegally-built extra floors at the factory collapsed, killing 64 workers. This resulted in our building a nascent programme specifying what we would expect brands to do to prevent disasters. There were further tragedies, such as the fire at the Tazreen factory in 2012. We tried to push a compensation formula paid by the government and brands.

When Rana Plaza happened, it was off the scale – 1,134 garment workers died. Everyone was talking about it; even people on the bus were talking about it. The high media profile and public outcry forced brands to engage with what had happened. Over a million people wrote to H&M demanding that they sign the Accord; that was instrumental in getting other brands to sign. The same goes for compensation: we needed that attention to get the political will of the international community and to get the International Labour Organization and brands to sit down at the table. The Accord has helped to set standards for the industry, but no factory owner has been prosecuted yet for their illegal factory buildings.

What do you think of the Modern Slavery Act and what is needed to give it teeth?

The Act proves that it is possible to have regulatory and mandatory reporting, and that's an important principle to have won. But we need to push that principle to get brands to report on and publish the list of their suppliers, and to go a step further than their competitors. We need to be sure that these reports are accurate and that they drive change on the ground for the workers. We need these reports to be translated, displayed and presented in a way that is useful for the public.

There is a grey area between slavery and exploitation. The migration of workers is not human trafficking, but I have seen how they are trapped in the same way as people who are trafficked. They are recruited from their home villages; they often sell their land and then travel huge distances and are so heavily in debt that they can't go back home. We don't want people to say that if you're not a slave then technically you're okay. The victims of Rana Plaza went to work even though they knew that it was unsafe, because they had no choice; they couldn't afford to go without their monthly pay. There needs to be more regulation, and CEOs and company boards need to be held legally accountable for the exploitation and slavery that they are allowing to happen.

cleanclothes.org

An opportunity to strengthen the law

In July 2016, I went to meet Baroness Lola Young at the House of Lords in London to discuss her important role in shaping the Modern Slavery Act. A member of the House of Lords since 2004, she is an independent crossbench peer who has been involved in many campaigns to criminalize and combat modern forms of enslavement.

How did you come to work on the Modern Slavery Act?

Liberty and Anti-Slavery International approached me to introduce a clause criminalizing forced labour and domestic servitude, which was eventually enacted through the Coroners and Justice Act in 2009. At that time, few seemed to recognize the extent to which a modern form of slavery was happening here in Britain.

In 2015, the government decided to consolidate and expand legislation in this area. Colleagues from ethical and sustainable fashion that I'd been working with alerted me to the potential of Section 54 of the Modern Slavery Bill. The proposed clause required companies trading in the UK with a turnover of £36 million [$45 million] or more to make a statement on their efforts to rid their supply chains of slave labour. We realized that here was an opportunity to strengthen the law and to make it more robust, especially with regard to the fashion industry.

There has been growing concern, partly from investors, to make sure they aren't profiting from others' misery. Most of the best-loved, most-respected high-street names support these measures. Why should those with dodgy practices in their supply chains gain commercial advantage with their low prices and cavalier attitudes to people employed in their supply chains? The benefits of a level playing field, where companies are held to account for their business practices, are obvious.

What could undermine The Modern Slavery Act?

I suspect that this law will eventually need further strengthening. At the moment, it's possible to produce a statement in which a company effectively says it hasn't done anything to examine its supply chain. That's not right, it's a cop-out. Another challenge is already manifesting itself: statements written according to templates provided by a 'consultant' that are all very similar.

In 2016 you proposed an amendment to the Act. Why was that?

Before the Act was passed, we had tried to insert a clause to include public bodies in Section 54. At the moment, it only refers to commercial companies, and we feel this is not logical. My Private Member's Bill – essentially an amendment to the Modern Slavery Act – requires public bodies to publish a yearly statement on how they are eliminating modern slavery from their supply chains. It would require the government to publish a list of companies that should be complying with the law.

Janie Airey

"It would be really helpful for concerned consumers and those campaigning for change to have a central, web-based repository housing all the anti-modern slavery statements."

There has been a big movement to incorporate Fair Trade products in public-sector procurement too. Is that progressing?

Yes. We need to promote best practice; NGOs and the public are increasingly agitating for more transparency. We want to know that what we buy isn't causing misery, or even loss of life. The NHS and local authorities can be very influential with regard to procurement of services. The combined purchasing power of this sector is £45 billion [$56 billion].

What was your personal motivation to get the amendment to the Modern Slavery Act to bring about transparency in supply chains?

I don't want to feel that my buying habits damage anyone trying to earn a living, whether that's in the UK or overseas. The California Transparency in Supply Chains Act [see page 24] was a source of inspiration, showing what could be achieved. I think we've built on this, but there's much to do. For example, President Obama's Executive Order set a high standard for procurement through federal contracts.

I love fashion and I've noticed a significant increase in companies seeking advice and support, wanting to get this right. We have to push on and encourage companies to work together to sign up to common values and practices in the industry. My fear is that another disaster on the scale of the Rana Plaza tragedy may be just around the corner.

How can we fast forward the transition the fashion industry needs to make?

We need to develop a package of support to help both the workers and the fashion industry. We need to think about what kind of fashion industry we want in the future. Our government should be working with other states to promote responsible, accountable business. Using international bodies such as the EU, the UN and the Commonwealth, as well as trading partnerships brokered by the World Trade Organization, should be high up the political agenda.

Corporate leadership on modern slavery

"The Modern Slavery Act has been a game-changer. Seventy-seven per cent of companies think there is a likelihood of modern slavery occurring in their supply chain. CEO engagement with modern slavery has doubled. Boards of directors are being trained on modern slavery risks and 50 per cent of companies are collaborating more with peers, NGOs and multi-stakeholder initiatives. A new quality of leadership is emerging."

Quintin Lake, Research Fellow, Hult International Business School

Having personally led People Tree, a social business dedicated to Fair Trade, in developing processes to monitor positive social impact and risks, I find it fascinating to see how the more advanced companies are now putting processes in place to respond to the Modern Slavery Act.

Understanding and measuring the impact of the Modern Slavery Act is key to its ongoing development and success. To this end, the Ethical Trading Initiative and Ashridge/Hult International Business School compiled an in-depth analysis of business perspectives on tackling modern slavery: the Corporate Leadership on Modern Slavery Report (nin.tl/ashridge-hult).

Amongst other things, the report highlighted that:
- The Modern Slavery Act has been a game-changer.
- Addressing modern slavery is becoming a critical issue for businesses wishing to maintain credibility with customers, investors, NGOs and the general public.
- Senior leadership engagement is vital.
- Collaboration and partnerships are the way forward.

I went to meet Quintin Lake, who worked on the report. 'When the Modern Slavery Act was announced,' Quintin told me, 'our initial task was to help the thousands of companies reporting on their supply chains for the first time to learn from those who had been doing it for longer. Even companies that had been looking at ethical trade and ethical sourcing for a long time, with human rights approaches that ran throughout their business around due diligence of supply and supplier standards, realized they needed to go beyond codes of conduct and audit programmes.

Long-term partnerships between brands and suppliers promote better working conditions, wages and environmental standards. These women work at Stylus Printers in India.

Miki Alcalde

'Bonded labour, forced overtime and child labour require a wider scope than just checking the general standards within factories. Factory owners go to great lengths to keep illegal workers hidden. There was double book-keeping, buzzers on reception to alert illegal workers to leave the building via the back door when the auditors arrived, that sort of thing.'

I asked Quintin what corporate leaders need to do to tackle slavery.

'Senior leaders set the tone that everyone else follows in the business,' he replied. 'Tackling modern slavery means really getting to know your supply chain. Where are the areas of their sourcing or production in which people could be being exploited? Leadership needs to be much more strategic – it is not just a CSR [corporate social responsibility] skill set.

'We also saw in our report that the passion, skill and ability of the person charged with leading this response to eradicate modern slavery – whether they report directly to the board or not – is critical. We saw a marked distinction in the quality of the organization's response to modern slavery linked to the quality of the person leading that change.

'Companies are extremely cautious about how much they should share publicly about the risk of modern slavery, or report on modern slavery cases found in their supply chains. They worry that campaigning NGOs and the media will exploit this to "name and shame" their company.

'Companies we spoke to welcomed pro-active engagement from NGOs and customers – to challenge and stretch them – and also stated that they wanted to

Miki Alcalde

find more ways to work collaboratively with the media to highlight key issues. But they feel there needs to be a greater public understanding of the complexity of issues before they can be fully transparent about what they are finding.' This will also help less-advanced companies to progress in their journey to eradicate modern slavery.

Most of the more advanced companies cited remediation mechanisms and key performance indicators that focus on impacts to improve conditions for workers, yet fewer than 37 per cent of companies had these in place. We still have a long way to go!

Helping to keep these issues on the agenda of businesses and in the public consciousness are organizations such as the Ethical Trading Initiative, which play an important facilitating role in the fight to eradicate modern slavery and to improve working conditions for millions.

The Ethical Trade Initiative

The Ethical Trade Initiative (ETI) is an alliance of companies, trade unions and NGOs that work together to promote respect for workers' rights around the globe. It aims to create a world where all workers are free from exploitation and discrimination, and enjoy freedom, security and equity. The Modern Slavery Act has given the ETI momentum as the leading business platform for companies, trade unions and NGOs, as it facilitates know-how and leadership to help members and businesses to improve their practices and eradicate slavery.

The ETI was started in the early 1990s, at a time when the first generation of ethical consumers were shocked to read news of sweatshop conditions and exploitation in the clothing and footwear factories of southeast Asia. Consumers got active, and companies started to adopt codes of conduct

"The UN's Guiding Principles on Business and Human Rights are a transformational road map to a future where the billions of people whose lives are impacted by corporate activities are treated with respect for their dignity and fundamental welfare – a world where human beings and corporations alike can thrive and prosper."

John Ruggie, author of the *UN Guiding Principles on Business and Human Rights*, which calls on companies to respect and support the Universal Declaration of Human Rights and ensure they are not complicit in human rights abuses.

in response. These were voluntary and largely ineffective; they were widely criticized for lacking credibility. In 1997 a group of companies, trade unions and NGOs identified the need for an organization to establish consistent standards and guidance for ethical trade to combine the authority and expertise of the trade-union and campaign movements with the practical know-how and buying power of big businesses. In 1998, the ETI was created by a small group of visionaries who believed in the power of collective action to make a difference to the lives of workers in companies' supply chains. Pioneers like The Body Shop and Sainsbury's joined the ETI in 1998; there are now over 115 members. Together, they have the power to improve the lives of over 10 million workers around the world.

When companies join the ETI, they sign up to the ETI Base Code (see page 23), which is based on the International Labour Organization (ILO) Conventions – an internationally recognized set of labour standards.

In 2015, the ETI was closely involved in shaping the Modern Slavery Act. In particular, it persuaded the government to focus on supply chains and labour exploitation; issues that initially found no mention in the Act because the government assumed that industry did not want to be burdened with regulation. At this stage, the government believed that voluntary standards and challenges from civil society would be more than enough to make business behave more ethically. However, this was not the case and business

lobbied government for a legislative requirement for commercial companies to provide slavery and human-trafficking statements, in order to create a level playing field so that they would not be at a disadvantage as they improved practice.

In an interview with OpenDemocracy, Cindy Berman, head of knowledge and learning at the ETI, explained how the Act came into being:

'Rana Plaza was a game-changer for many companies... We are looking at issues of choice for workers who wanted to leave an environment that they felt was unsafe yet were desperate to earn wages, almost at any cost. There is extreme vulnerability of those workers, and I think it forced many of our members, and the business community, especially in the retail sector, to take note.

'Good practice can only happen when there is a level playing field. This is created by government regulation and legislation; without this, businesses are competing in an unfair market.

'ETI members (businesses, trade unions and NGOs) signed a letter to government showing overwhelming support for a clause demanding transparency in the supply chain to be added to the Modern Slavery Act.

'I think that really did shift the needle, despite the fact that MPs and NGOs had been haranguing and engaging for a long time. The government really needed to get that message from industry.'

I went to meet Cindy Berman to hear more about what ETI members are doing to address modern slavery in their supply chains.

It is good to see that some ETI members have their top-tier suppliers listed on their websites. What are the next steps?

We expect our members to progressively map their supply chains all the way down and, where possible and appropriate, to make these public. Some members have over 35,000 supply chains, so we don't expect this to happen all at once. That said, supply-chain transparency is important, but it is not the only way of improving ethical trade practices.

What obstacles do companies face in eradicating slave labour further down their supply chains?

Challenges include limited leverage (i.e. where they are purchasing a small percentage of a supplier's product and therefore have limited influence in changing and improving labour practices) and sub-contracting, in which companies are not aware that their orders have been passed on to another factory.

In your experience, what kind of slavery is most common in the fashion supply chain?

The risk of slavery is to be found in places where there is a high prevalence of migrant or precarious labour, discrimination or high unemployment, or where governments are either unwilling or lack the resources or capacity to regulate and monitor working conditions. This could be anywhere – we know that there are increasing numbers of workers in modern slavery in the UK and other countries in Europe, as well as in places like Turkey where there is a high number of Syrian refugees. We have also learnt that, in places like Malta, state-sponsored slavery, involving North Korean workers, has been found in factories that supply well-known brands.

What captures the imagination of the public most when it comes to modern slavery?

Unfortunately it is the shocking stories, the exposés in the media that most capture public imagination. I hope that we will start to see a more sophisticated conversation in the public domain about the growing consumer demand for ever-decreasing prices and instantly available goods.

How would you build on the transparency clause in the Modern Slavery Act in order to give it more power?

The legislation is currently light-touch and requires only that companies publish a statement on the steps they are taking to prevent modern slavery and manage the risks. The minimum we need right now is for the government to publish a list of companies that are required to report. Without that, it is impossible for anyone to know who is or is not complying with the law. And I would like the government to insist that all Modern Slavery Statements are published in a central repository where they can be held up for scrutiny by government, investors, civil society and the public at large.

Next, I would like to see the Act including all public-procurement systems, and public bodies to be bound by the same legislation. And, down the line, I'd like to see strengthened legislation requiring companies to take effective action where the risks or incidence of modern slavery are found.

ethicaltrade.org

ETI Base Code

Employment is freely chosen
Slavery and bonded labour are totally unacceptable. Almost 21 million people are victims of forced labour.

Freedom of association and the right to collective bargaining are respected
Tens of thousands of workers lose their jobs every year for attempting to form or join a trade union or improve working conditions.

Working conditions are safe and hygienic
An estimated 2.3 million people die every year from work-related accidents and diseases.

Child labour shall not be used
168 million children work to support their families, missing out on education and often damaging their health. This reinforces the cycle of poverty.

Living wages are paid
Roughly half the world's population still lives on two dollars a day. If people can't feed their families on an adult's wage, they may send their children to work.

Working hours are not excessive
Long working hours are the norm for most of the world's workers. This damages people's health and undermines family life.

No discrimination is practised
Women and certain minorities are often confined to the lowest-paid jobs with no access to training or promotion.

Regular employment is provided
Most workers can be laid off when it suits the employer. This fuels poverty and insecurity and drives down wages.

No harsh or inhumane treatment is allowed
Few workers have protection against physical, verbal or sexual abuse in the workplace.

Making transparency work

Three years before the advent of Britain's Modern Slavery Act, the California Transparency in Supply Chains Act came into law, providing consumers in this US state with important information about the business practices of their favourite brands.

The 2012 law, which applies to any company with a turnover of $100 million or more, means that companies must disclose the efforts they are making to prevent and root out human trafficking and slavery in their product supply chains, both locally and overseas.

Ben Skinner, the founder of Transparentem, a non-profit that uses investigative reporting to stop environmental and human rights abuses, travelled the globe to research his book about modern-day slavery, *A Crime So Monstrous*. He told me more about the California Transparency Act and its impact so far.

How do the California Act and the UK Modern Slavery Act compare?

There are two major advantages of the Modern Slavery Act that jump out at me. The first is that the disclosures require sign-off by the company's board, which increases the level of responsibility and awareness at the very top. As it stands, too many boards of directors of major companies are purposely kept in the dark about many of the potential dangers upstream in their supply chain.

The second advantage is an accidental one, in that one of its champions was Theresa May, who had been outspoken on human trafficking as Home Secretary. So you now have a prime minister who should be doing everything to enforce it.

Enforcement is the challenge. As with any kind of legislation, it's only as good as the accurate and actionable intelligence that is brought to law enforcement's attention. There's lots of conjecture about what goes on upstream, but it takes real effort to find the current connections between actual forced labour and the brands and retailers that are selling products made in part or in whole with slavery.

What success has the California Transparency in Supply Chains Act had?

It is a disclosure act. There are no requirements beyond disclosure. If a retailer, seller or manufacturer has an annual turnover of $100 million and does even $1 of business in the state of California, that company is required to put a statement on its corporate website. A company can decide what level of detail it goes into. It can simply say: 'We don't know what's in our supply chain, we don't use third-party auditors to check our supply chains, we cannot guarantee to any of our customers that we are selling them slave-free products.' A company can say that and still be compliant with the Act.

If a company is wilfully not putting anything on their website, in theory the California Attorney General can go after them. Also, if they falsely disclose, there is potential for civil litigation. In practice, their disclosures, like the disclosures to investors for conflict minerals, are usually framed in language like: 'We make every effort to understand what's going on upstream, but from time to time our suppliers are not totally transparent and we can't guarantee a slave-free supply chain.' However, the Act has given customers a tool to potentially make decisions.

What do you think will further help eradicate slavery and exploitation in supply chains?
The closure of the Section 307 loophole is probably the most important piece of recent US legislation. When President Obama closed the consumptive demand loophole in the Tariff Act in February 2016, the US got a powerful tool to protect consumers from being sold slave-made goods. It remains to be seen if President Trump will use it to fulfil his duty to protect those consumers – and American workers who would otherwise be competing with products made by child slaves.

Are we seeing citizens in California making a noise and putting pressure on companies?
The most effective campaigns are based on hard data upstream. For example, if you know that cotton is being produced by forced labour in Uzbekistan and you can verifiably trace all the way upstream from the bales, then you have the opportunity to build a credible and actionable campaign. Consumers must demand transparency from brands – this will keep the pressure up.

What are your plans for Transparentem?
Transparentem is a non-profit organization that helps to understand what goes on upstream in corporate supply chains. We want to give brands actionable information. Regardless of their action or non-action, the information will eventually enter a continuum of disclosure that may include their investors, regulators, and a select number of experienced journalists. We use best practice as governed under the Code of Ethics for the Society of Professional Journalists to understand the full picture. We are trying to find systemic problems that affect the lives of thousands of people. We start upstream, and don't target any brands in particular.

transparentem.com

"Do you want to shop from a brand that values transparency? From a company that is constantly pushing the agenda to a better understanding of what's happening? Or do you want to shop with a company that takes a hands-off attitude with its suppliers and doesn't give a damn about human rights in its supply chain?"

Ben Skinner, founder, Transparentem

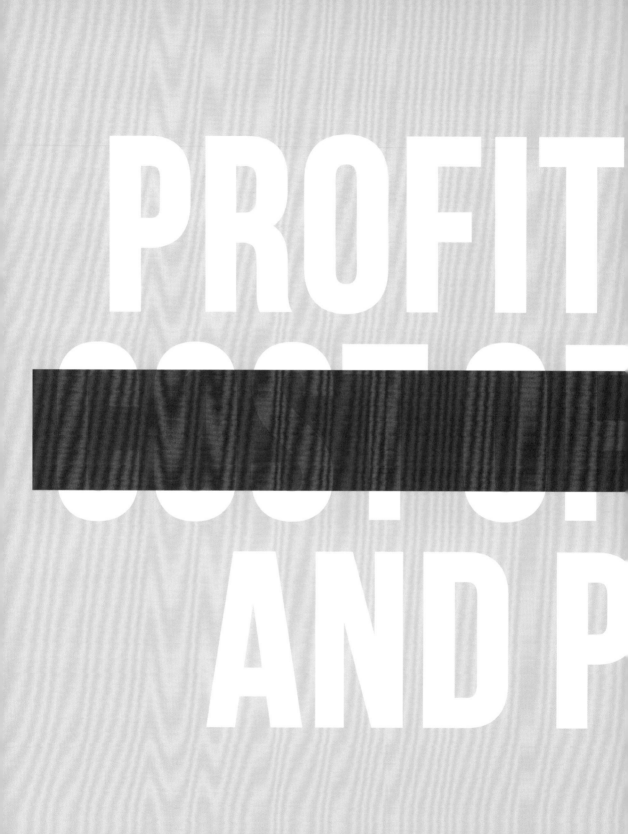

PROFIT

AND P

AT THE
PEOPLE
PLANET

THE GLOBAL ECONOMY AND THE FASHION INDUSTRY

Fashion, the world's third-largest industry after cars and electronics, and the second most-polluting industry in the world after oil, has a major impact on millions of workers and on the environment.

Miki Alcalde

Delhi, India – no accountability means workers toil late into the night to finish orders.

The Fair Trade, social-justice and trade-union movements, SDGs and other global initiatives have paved the way to protect workers' rights in the supply chain, but corporations now have more power than governments.

The fashion industry directly employs 60 million people, and about double that number are thought to be indirectly dependent on the clothing industry for their work. The Fairtrade Foundation estimates that as many as 100 million households are directly engaged in growing cotton, with a further 300 million people involved in processing and transporting it.

With an estimated worth of $3,000 billion, the global fashion industry, which includes clothes, textiles, footwear and luxury goods, has huge commercial and financial power. Fashion's profitability, growth and reach have outstripped high-growth sectors such as technology and communications, and it is now shaping wider cultural trends, including our identity, attitudes, behaviour and beliefs. There has never been a more urgent need to change the fashion industry to one that feeds and empowers our growing global population while also finding environmental solutions to climate change and depleting water supplies.

Trade, not aid

The fight for fairer trade and social justice began with grassroots civil-society movements. In the 1980s, 'Trade, not aid' was the call: fair business practices would allow people in the developing world to trade their way out of hunger and poverty, rather than being reliant on charity. But the problem for developing countries was that, although international trade grew, the West found ways to 'stitch up' trade rules to favour their corporations. Despite the competitive advantage that developing countries have in terms of low cost of living and cheaper labour relative to Western countries, the developing world still found it difficult to access markets. One example of this 'stitch-up' that still exists today is the subsidies paid to cotton farmers by wealthy Western

UNIVERSITY OF WINCHESTER
LIBRARY

> "There needs to be a paradigm shift in terms of the responsibility of brands to protect and be accountable to every single person in the supply chain. We don't just want to see best practice... there needs to be binding accountability."
>
> John Hilary, former Executive Director of War on Want

governments to protect their own industry. This policy keeps cotton prices artificially low, meaning that cotton farmers in poorer countries find it hard to compete and survive. The rules of trade need to be fair and change in favour of the most economically marginalized people throughout the world.

The revival of rural hand skills
Prices have also fallen dramatically compared to 40 years ago.
A world population that has grown from 4.5 billion in 1980 to 7.5 billion today has created a huge unskilled population that is desperate for work. I feel passionately that we need a new type of fashion industry that has at its heart an understanding of our growing human population and our planet's limited resources. We need to create textiles and clothing using the maximum amount of labour (through sustainable farming practices and manufacturing, and paying producers decently) while using as few natural resources as possible.

The production process – from growing fibre for fabrics, to fabric dyeing and printing – needs to use renewable energy or human hands and to pollute as little as possible. The gold benchmark of fashion should be a contemporary Gandhian model, with self-sustaining communities producing crafted textiles and printed and embellished fabrics using organic, GM-free, Fair Trade cotton and other natural fibres with a low environmental impact. Fashion brands and governments need to invest in this bottom tier of the fashion supply chain in order to promote livelihoods and create jobs in rural areas – perhaps small factories and workshops next to the organic fields of cotton and local food crops.

We need to be more discerning in our purchasing: buying new items less often and, when we do buy, opting for a mixture of ethically and fairly produced clothing from large factories and items produced in smaller workplaces using artisanal craft skills such as hand-woven fabrics, hand embellishment and hand knitting.

What is the true cost of labour?
Today, a whole generation of shoppers expect to be able to buy cheap clothing – but these low prices are only possible because of the slavery and exploitation that exist in the fashion supply chain. The price of clothes does not reflect the true cost to the farmers, spinners and weavers, tailors, finishers, quality-control teams and packers who are underpaid and overworked in the race to get the latest fashion items into our stores. Many of them are forced to live and work in shocking conditions, as you will learn when we meet some of these people in Chapter 3. Workers in developing countries are often left helpless by lack of workplace representation and unions that could speak up for their rights. As a result, we are witnessing a global 'race to the bottom', with developing countries competing against each other to supply the cheapest labour in a bid to attract brands to their factories. Business operations and corporate practices are driven by the constant search for low-input prices, high profits and shorter lead times, which increases the risk of worker exploitation and of slavery. Allowing freedom of association and paying living wages is key to changing the status quo (see pages 42 and 44).

Sustainable Development Goals

In September 2015, 193 countries signed up to 17 UN Sustainable Development Goals (SDGs) – an ambitious agenda for social, economic and environmental improvement across the globe. These goals build on the Millennium Development Goals, which, while inspiring the social sector, seemed of limited interest to business. The problems of poverty-induced modern slavery and climate change are now so bad that 'business as usual'

can't continue, and the SDGs provide us with a full road map for change. They cover key concepts such as decent livelihoods, education, health, poverty and gender equality, but they also have strong environmental principles that reflect our urgent need to switch from fossil fuels to renewable energy and to conserve water.

sustainabledevelopment.un.org

Setting the agenda for Fair Trade

The World Fair Trade Organization (WFTO)

For over 30 years, the Fair Trade movement has been leading by example: proving that better trade can empower the poor, and showing mainstream businesses how to do business with people and the environment at its heart. Fair Trade started as a citizens' action in the developed world in response to poverty, hunger and injustice in the developing world. People understood that unfair trade was the cause of human rights violations and that, as consumers, they could be part of the solution by buying Fair Trade products. Thousands of micro-economic, practical, Fair Trade and social-business solutions sprang up worldwide.

Fair Trade goes beyond reducing risk and harm to workers and the environment; it seeks to empower workers economically by bringing trade to the most marginalized people, especially women. It is based on long-term relationships which strengthen suppliers and enable meaningful and sustainable social impact. Fair Trade is a trading partnership based on dialogue, transparency and respect, that promotes livelihoods, cultural and traditional skills, and self-determination, and helps with pre-finance where needed. The Fair Trade movement has campaigned against child labour and all forms of exploitation, and for child education and decent adult wages, through local initiatives and through public policy.

Fair Trade makes the principles of people and planet central to business operations. This influences all decisions in design, buying, operations, marketing and communications. Fair Trade groups are working with leading institutions to promote new accounting methods based on the triple bottom line (people, plant and profit), new economic indicators, ethical standards in agriculture and manufacture, in worker participation and gender equality, new approaches to finance, public awareness, and creating new demand and markets for ethical products.

wfto.com

Rudi Dalvai, President of the World Fair Trade Organization, explains how its principles link to other international standards:

1 The Sustainable Development Goals (SDGs) are clearly linked to the WFTO Fair Trade Principles. For example, it is in our DNA to follow sustainable production and consumption as set out in SDG12. The SDGs have given international authority to our approach to trading and business. They underline the fact that governments now realize much of the work championed by the Fair Trade movement is essential to building the future of humanity.

2 The Fair Trade movement welcomes the Modern Slavery Act and corporations becoming more transparent – we want 100 per cent of trade to be Fair Trade. The *True Cost* movie [truecostmovie.com] showed the reality of the fashion industry. The distance between Fair Trade standards and principles and what conventional companies are doing is huge. Fair Trade is way beyond Corporate Social Responsibility.

3 Fair Trade has also helped start the debate about the exploitation of workers here in Europe – like the use of migrant workers harvesting tomatoes in southern Italy – yet our supermarkets continue their irresponsible buying practices.

4 Fair Trade can change the world on a micro-economic level. Then it is up to labour unions, governments and international agencies to ensure business is done responsibly and slavery is no longer a reality.

The Fair Trade towns movement sends a message.

WFTO 10 Principles of Fair Trade

The World Fair Trade Organization (WFTO) has created 10 principles that Fair Trade organizations must follow in their day-to-day work. WFTO carries out monitoring to ensure these principles are maintained. Over 400 Fair Trade organizations and producers are members. WFTO was established in 1986.

For a fairer world
WFTO's members commit to 10 Principles of Fair Trade in their daily business practices (see right). Our vision is a world in which trade structures and practices have been transformed to correct the imbalances in the global economy that leave communities and cultures impoverished and drive environmental and economic catastrophe.

WFTO connects and provides a network for business and organizations in the supply chain to exchange innovative ideas and best practices. We work together to provide a solution for humane, sustainable global trading by creating synergies to advance Fair Trade.

"The World Fair Trade Organization and I have a long association! I remember running around its Biennial Conference, in Milan, in 1999, trying to get another 20 signatories in order to have a democratic chance of formalizing a special day for Fair Trade. We succeeded, and World Fair Trade Day was born. It is now celebrated around the world on the second Saturday of May each year."

Safia Minney

01 – Creating Opportunities for Economically Disadvantaged Producers

Fair Trade is a strategy for poverty alleviation and sustainable development. Its purpose is to create opportunities for producers who have been economically disadvantaged or marginalized by the conventional trading system.

02 – Transparency & Accountability

Fair Trade involves transparent management and commercial relations to deal fairly and respectfully with trading partners.

03 – Trade Relations

Fair Trade organizations trade with concern for the social, economic and environmental well-being of marginalized small producers and do not maximize profit at their expense. They maintain long-term relationships based on solidarity, trust and mutual respect that contribute to the promotion and growth of Fair Trade. An interest-free pre-payment of at least 50 per cent is made if requested.

04 – Payment of a Fair Price

A fair price in the regional or local context is one that has been agreed through dialogue and participation. It covers not only the costs of production but enables production which is socially just and environmentally sound. It provides fair pay to the producers, and takes into account the principle of equal pay for equal work by women and men. Fair Traders ensure prompt payment to their partners and, whenever possible, help producers with access to pre-harvest or pre-production financing.

05 – Child Labour

Fair Trade organizations respect the UN Convention on the Rights of the Child, as well as local laws and social norms in order to ensure that the participation of children in production processes of fairly traded articles (if any) does not adversely affect their well-being, security, educational requirements and need for play. Organizations working directly with informally organized producers disclose the involvement of children in production.

06 – Non-Discrimination, Gender Equity and Freedom of Association

The organization does not discriminate in hiring, remuneration, access to training, promotion, termination or retirement based on race, caste, national origin, religion, disability, gender, sexual orientation, union membership, political affiliation, HIV/AIDS status or age. Fair Trade means that women's work is properly valued and rewarded. Women are always paid for their contribution to the production process and are empowered in their organizations.

07 – Working Conditions

Fair Trade means a safe and healthy working environment for producers. Working hours and conditions comply with conditions established by national and local laws and International Labour Organization conventions.

08 – Capacity Building

Fair Trade is a means to develop producers' independence. Fair Trade relationships provide continuity, during which producers and their marketing organizations can improve their management skills and their access to new markets.

09 – Promoting Fair Trade

Fair Trade organizations raise awareness of Fair Trade and the possibility of greater justice in world trade. They provide their customers with information about the organization, the products, and in what conditions they are made. They use honest advertising and marketing techniques, and aim for the highest standards in product quality and packing.

10 – The Environment

Fair Trade actively encourages better environmental practices and the application of responsible methods of production and consumption.

The Fairtrade Foundation

Established in 1992, this is a non-profit organization that licenses use of the FAIRTRADE Mark on products in accordance with internationally agreed Fairtrade standards. The standards include protection of workers' rights and the environment, payment of the Fairtrade Minimum Price and an additional Fairtrade Premium to invest in business or community projects. Buying products with the FAIRTRADE Mark supports small-scale farmers and workers – among the most marginalized groups globally – through trade rather than aid, to enable them to maintain their livelihoods and reach their potential.

Mike Gidney, Chief Executive of the Fairtrade Foundation, has been a long-time friend of mine since his days running the Fairtrade Advocacy office for Traidcraft. We caught up to discuss how the Fairtrade movement is continuing to set the agenda for better business practice in the UK and globally.

What impact has the Fairtrade Foundation had?

The Fairtrade Foundation has connected with consumers and set the standard for what they expect from companies in tackling inequality previously hidden in their supply chains. Fairtrade and the Ethical Trade Initiative (ETI) were established as different, sister initiatives around the same time, so we've 'grown up together' and been able to learn from and reinforce each other, as well as collaborate on issues such as living wages, the Modern Slavery Act and improving audit methodologies.

It would be hard to think of another initiative that has done more than Fairtrade over the past 20 years to put justice in business supply chains and create the groundswell of public and consumer pressure – from very local communities through to major business networks. It is gratifying to see issues such as smallholder agriculture (SDG2), decent work (SDG8) and sustainable consumption and production (SDG12) now a key part of the global framework for tackling inequality and for sustainable development (see page 31).

We have seen an increase in interest from people asking for greater transparency in regard to where their food has come from. I think the rise in companies wanting to work with Fairtrade, be it through putting the Mark on their products or entering into a partnership with us, shows that many companies have taken this need for fairness on board in order to give the public the confidence and reassurance they need about how their product is produced.

What is the Fairtrade Foundation's involvement with the Modern Slavery Act?

The Home Office originally didn't want to include a 'transparency in supply chains' measure in the draft Bill, but only wanted this to be done through voluntary organizations and statements – it was due to the intervention of organizations like the ETI, Fairtrade Foundation, Anti-Slavery International, the Corporate Responsibility Coalition and our business and retail partners that we managed to achieve this development, recognizing that forced labour and modern slavery are criminal acts, and smart regulation to drive a consistent business-responsible approach and level playing field was needed.

In a similar way, we worked alongside other British NGOs to push for the establishment of a Grocery Code Adjudicator (GCA), or supermarket watchdog, recognizing the power of retailers regarding their supply chain and the need for their suppliers to be dealt with fairly, so that excessive risk to workers is not passed down the supply chain. We are currently feeding into the review of the GCA role and remit, and calling for expansion so that an ability to appeal to the GCA is not just for first-tier suppliers, but allows the GCA to investigate deeper into supply chains and complaints from primary producers.

As the mainstream begins to pursue a radical transparency and improve conditions for workers, how can Fairtrade compete and continue to set the agenda?

Fairtrade has always been about pushing for change, not accepting the norm but adapting and innovating in order to drive lasting, sustainable change for the farmers and workers in its system. However, we also see our standards as the minimum a company should be doing – which is why we are still calling on firms to do more. We are seeing companies say they want to work with us to achieve more, and our strategy is to expand our offer to business, to work with them to drive greater impact and greater lasting change.

"Fairtrade has always been about pushing for change, not accepting the norm but adapting and innovating in order to drive lasting, sustainable change... Minimum standards are just the beginning – we need to create a race to the top."

Mike Gidney, Chief Executive of the Fairtrade Foundation

Minimum standards are just the beginning – we need to create a race to the top.

The area of transparency that remains so difficult to crack is that of publishing what you pay. Fairtrade has been a true radical here, with published minimum pricing and premium structures. Lots of companies now claim to benchmark themselves to our standards, or even claim to pay above Fairtrade minimums, but where is the evidence, and who is checking? Workers can now upload their pay slip on WhatsApp, or use it to expose the living conditions in a factory dormitory as evidence of unfair treatment, so it's going to be increasingly difficult for companies to cover up what is really happening in their supply chains. While we understand the need for commercial confidentiality, the era of radical transparency is coming ever closer on these matters, whether through social-media networking and new IT platforms, or new supply-chain trading and transparency mechanisms such as Blockchain [database] now appearing. It's a good thing and companies should embrace it.

What's next for the Fairtrade Foundation?
Our five-year strategy, 'Fairtrade can, I can' sets out our goals to 2020. What has been clear to us is that as companies get involved with Fairtrade they often realize they have more to do to drive real, lasting, sustainable change. We need to embed a commitment to fair trading deep within the operating model and governance of companies, not just as an add-on, and so we will broaden the ways we work with companies to achieve real impact. And we need to deepen the emotional connection with the public, especially given the rise of nationalism and populism. We cannot turn inward and protect our own economies at the expense of marginalized producers who, though out of sight, must never be out of mind.

Over the next five years we will see a targeted ramping-up of Fairtrade Foundation support for cocoa, coffee, banana, tea and flower producers to create a lasting sustainable impact. We want to work with more companies to tackle the issues they face today and tomorrow, be it access to workers' rights and welfare, a living wage or mitigating the impact of climate change. We are also keen to develop Fairtrade Foundation's public pull, to mobilize the extraordinary public support that has sustained us over the years, to increase demand for Fairtrade and trade justice, particularly as the UK looks to develop new trade deals and policies that could affect the business, social and environmental regulations previously led by Europe.

fairtrade.org.uk

The need to organize

When in the early 1990s I read about sweatshops and exploited garment workers making our clothes, I started to design Fair Trade clothes. Putting together the first collections meant finding partner Fair Trade groups and setting up the first Fair Trade supply chains. I realized I also needed to know what the reality was for garment workers, so that I could make sure Fair Trade addressed the problems they faced. The search for answers brought me into contact with Amirul Haque Amin, Executive Director of the National Garment Workers Federation (NGWF).

The NGWF is the largest national trade union in Bangladesh. For more than 30 years, it has been fighting for the rights of garment workers. The country's ready-made garment industry is now the second-largest in the world and has become a key driver of the economy and the nation's development. It employs around four million workers, of whom 55 to 60 per cent are women, according to the International Labour Organization. Exports of mass-produced clothing totalled $24.5 billion in 2013/14, accounting for over 80 per cent of the nation's export earnings.

NGWF is demanding:
- Living wages: we want to ensure a living wage for the workers. We do not have a specific figure, but the current [monthly] wage is about 5,000 taka [$63] and it should be closer to 10,000 taka [$126]. So it needs to double.
- The fundamental right for workers to organize themselves and bargain collectively.
- A tripartite advocation, consultation and monitoring committee between the brands, factory owners and trade unions.
- Safe workplaces.
- Equal rights for women.

The NGWF is strengthening the trade-union movement across Bangladesh by setting up factory-level unions that can challenge labour-rights abuses within factories. It also promotes workers' rights through targeted campaigning and by lobbying the government, factory owners and transnational corporations for stronger legislation and better enforcement of workplace laws. Amirul Haque Amin (pictured right leading the protest) is the Federation's president and co-founder, and recently became chair of IndustriALL. He says that, though the sector creates job opportunities for millions of people, workers are being highly exploited.

'Many work long hours,' he says. 'Legally they shouldn't work more than eight hours. Overtime is meant to be voluntary but for many factories two hours' overtime is mandatory. In some factories, workers work four, five or six hours' overtime. Excessive, compulsory overtime is slavery. If international companies became transparent, fair and responsible, slavery would stop.

Some major brands are now becoming more transparent, which is positive...
I cannot say that any brand is fully transparent. Some, like H&M, Zara and Gap, have started to disclose their first-tier suppliers. [But] in addition they all need to talk about their pricing and what they are paying local manufacturers. They also need to disclose the wages they pay to local workers. I do not know of a single brand that is talking about its pricing and payments.

But brands have huge buying power to negotiate prices to the detriment of workers' wages and rights, don't they?
I sit with the factory owners and I know the buyers are pressurizing local manufacturers to lower their prices. In the name of competition, brands say prices have to go down.

Amirul Haque Amin leads an NGWF protest.

Safia Minney

Unions and workers must ensure that factories recognize the bargaining power of workers. The workers and unions must be sure the workplace is safe. Brands must pay a fair price for the product and local businesses must ensure workers receive living wages.

How can Britain's Modern Slavery Act make a difference in Bangladesh? Have you seen any changes yet?

No, not yet – no major changes or positive initiatives. Many people do not even know about it. The UK government needs to inform other governments, like ours here in Bangladesh.

It is great that the Act covers the whole of a company's supply chain, not just the UK workers. I think it would be helpful if the Act stated that companies themselves had to inform all of their staff, from the very top down, about the Modern Slavery Act. That way, all the workers in the supply chain would be empowered with knowledge.

What about trading companies? It is difficult to put pressure on them to change.

Brands should do business directly with the factories, not through trading companies. Brands would then have more oversight of their supply chain. They would also be able to raise prices and pay workers more, as trading companies take their margins too.

What stands in the way of freedom of association?

Brands do. They don't want to use factories with trade unions in them. They are worried about ruining their business system, which relies on exploiting the workers. If factory workers were organized, this exploitation could not take place.

If brands worked with factories that allowed workers' organizations, would clothing prices go up?

I don't agree with the concept that, if there is a union, the prices to customers will increase. If the system becomes transparent and fair, and if the brand's profit and the local factory owner's profit are slightly reduced, wages could automatically improve without affecting consumers.

What motivated you to use your skills to fight for labour rights and become a unionist?

When I was at university, I was involved in student politics on the Left. To change society, you need to organize working people. I studied a bit of law so I could advise workers. My proudest moment is that workers now get a May Day holiday: this did not happen before I organized them. Nor were the workers getting a festival bonus. Most workers were not getting even one day's holiday a week when we started, but we managed to change that to some extent. Nowadays, many women workers get four months' maternity leave. As president of the NGWF, I feel very proud.

It is shocking that trade unionists around the world are still tortured and murdered for daring to take a stand...

Trade unionists face false claims against them and other forms of harassment. Consumers need to raise their voices in support of workers, so that they can exercise their rights. Sadly, I think that often consumers are not interested in finding out about the condition of workers or activists. All they are interested in is getting a cheap price. They need to change their attitude. They absolutely need to know the conditions in which their clothes were made and the conditions that activists have to operate under. Consumers in the West need to stand up for the workers and be their voice; they need to express their solidarity with the workers.

Amirul Haque Amin, President of the National Garment Workers Federation, and his team share the realities of modern slavery in the garment industry in Bangladesh.

Freedom of association

"It is only through organizing into trade unions that workers can stand up for themselves and enforce their rights locally. Rather than relying on auditors, or waiting for a brand's corporate social responsibility department to pay a flying visit to fix a problem, we need to create a proper structure of industrial relations. Then you would have a mechanism for workers to negotiate wages on an industry-wide basis and ensure they are paid."

Jenny Holdcroft, Assistant General Secretary, IndustriALL Global Union

All those fighting to end modern slavery – from civil society, trade unions, governments and businesses – are united in calling for every worker to have the freedom to join a union. It is only by being united that workers will be able to fight for their rights, for respect and protection in the workplace, and for the payment of a living wage. These rights are the foundation of humane business practice; without them a fair, equitable world is not possible. Enforcing laws and regulations that guarantee the protection of unions in the workplace is also vital.

Freedom of association means allowing trade unions into the workplace with the capacity to function as a voice of the workers. Trade-union representatives in factories and offices can hear grievances and talk to management to ensure steps are taken to deal with complaints. They can negotiate better pay and conditions for workers and help to create systems that address gender inequality and sexual harassment (one of the main reasons women give for leaving their jobs and forgoing any benefits accrued through length of service). The risk of modern slavery dramatically decreases in workplaces where trade unions are encouraged to operate. As the ETI explains, 'the single biggest factor that can contribute to ending extreme labour exploitation is to recognize workers' rights to organize.'

A democratic and accountable decision-making approach to business, such as that promoted by the Fair Trade movement, is a key factor in the 'social dialogue' being used in industrial relations today. This approach is helping forward-thinking fashion brands, with the help of trade unions and NGOs, truly to engage with their suppliers. Terms such as 'long-term partnership', 'freedom of association' and a 'fair and living wage', pioneered by Fair Trade organizations, are starting to be used in mainstream business vocabulary.

Homeworkers: protecting their rights

Fair Trade can protect homeworkers making products for the export market, such as these members of KTS, Nepal.

Jane Tate from HomeWorkers Worldwide shines a light on the scale of exploitation among homeworkers in the fashion industry.

Although not fitting neatly into the category of modern slavery, homeworkers are definitely 'unfree labour': they have little choice or bargaining power, and no mobility. HomeWorkers Worldwide has worked with homeworkers in many different parts of the world and there are common patterns, even though the local context varies.

Homeworking is almost always linked to women being tied to the home by their unpaid domestic work. Although homeworkers can be of any age, the most common age group is those with young children. Others may be taking care of sick or disabled partners or elderly relatives. At the same time, women often take the main responsibility for family expenses so, in addition to their unpaid work, they need an income.

Sometimes migrant women are subject to racist attacks or don't have correct documentation; once again, this causes them to 'hide', and they can easily be exploited.

In relation to global supply chains in the fashion industry, it is clear that homework and other informal employment (small workshops, casual work in factories etc) provide a low-cost and flexible workforce. When powerful retailers put pressure on suppliers to reduce costs and respond rapidly to changes in fashion or smaller orders, the costs are passed down to those working at the end of the chain who have little or no bargaining power.

homeworksww.org.uk

What is a living wage?

A living wage is the salary a worker requires in order to cover their basic needs, including adequate food, shelter, education, clothing and healthcare. It should be possible for a living wage to be earned in the course of a normal working week. However, wages in the garment industry invariably fall below this and may even fall short of the legal minimum wage if unscrupulous employers choose to ignore the law.

However, common sense tells us that paying a wage that is enough to live on is good for business, good for the individual and good for society. The implementation of a living wage would help some of the poorest people and countries in the world to promote development, gender equality and education for the next generation, as well as reviving the local garment industry in the developed world by reducing the difference in manufacturing costs between the Global North and South.

Furthermore, paying a living wage, and thereby lifting millions out of poverty, would significantly help in our efforts to eradicate modern slavery. In the next chapter, we will meet many victims of poverty: people who are enslaved by working intolerably long hours in order to make ends meet; children who are forced to work to support their family – thus losing their chance of an education and a better life; and young women sold into bonded labour or trafficked into the sex industry.

Initiatives such as The Asia Floor Wage Alliance and ACT (Action, Collaboration, Transformation), supported by the IndustriALL global union, are paving the way towards a living wage. Other multi-stakeholder initiatives, including the Fair Wear Foundation, are also shaping and inspiring better business practice. Freedom of association for workers and involvement by trade unions is key in the campaign for a living wage. 'The workforce needs collective power to demand decent wages,' says Sam Maher of the Clean Clothes Campaign. 'If an initiative doesn't involve trade unions or worker organizations, it won't effect change.'

In Cambodia, there has been a significant workers' movement and this has improved wages. Fast-fashion brands have started their own living-wage initiatives, but these are often productivity programmes, with living wages linked to meeting tougher (and sometimes unattainable) production targets, putting workers under extreme stress and resulting in more bullying and violence in the workplace.

When the quality of the finished product is impaired, workers are fined, with money docked from their wages. 'Brands also have programmes that may look charitable, such as teaching workers financial literacy, but that misses the point,' notes Sam Maher. 'Workers are not poor

THE ASIA FLOOR WAGE

(AFW) is calculated based on the following assumptions:

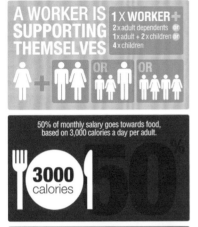

A WORKER IS SUPPORTING THEMSELVES — 1 X WORKER + 2 x adult dependents or 1 x adult + 2 x children or 4 x children

OR OR

50% of monthly salary goes towards food, based on 3,000 calories a day per adult.

3000 calories 50%

40% clothing, housing, travel costs, children's education, health costs.

40%

10% towards discretionary income (some entertainment, savings, pension or if main earner loses their job).

10%

www.cleanclothes.org

because they cannot manage their money; they are poor because they aren't paid properly.'

The Fair Wear Foundation has 85 member companies representing over 120 brands, such as TAKKO and Jack Wolfskin and pioneering ethical brand Nudie Jeans. In total, its members have 2,000 production locations and its members are working hard to make life better for thousands of workers, as its director, Erica Van Doorn, told me.

How does a living wage transform the lives of workers and their communities?

When people earn enough money, they don't have to work long overtime. And people who work 8 rather than 16 hours a day are more productive and make fewer mistakes – leading to better factory performance. Living wages lead to general improvements in workers' lives, from better nutrition to their children being able to go to school instead of helping support the family.

Who should pay the extra costs associated with a living wage?

The factory owner is only legally obliged to pay the minimum wage. Brands have been pushing prices down and because the factories need the business, they agree to the 'negotiated' prices. The factory owners then cut corners, and that's usually at the cost of the workers' wages. Buyers should make it possible to pay decent wages to the workers. Many brands state that they cannot pass on wage

increases to consumers because of the fierce competition, but they have mark-down sales of 30-40 per cent on clothing. They should try to reduce this instead, and pay the workers a living wage.

Buyers generally haven't got a clue what workers earn. Years ago, when production was in-house, buyers had the expertise to understand and calculate how many minutes go into production and multiply that by hourly earnings... now they don't. But change can come about with more buyer awareness. The Fair Wear Foundation's model of living-wage calculation is inspiring other initiatives to follow our wage ladder, which includes the Asia floor wage benchmark, and local trade-union and NGO calculations of a living wage. Governments, the Clean Clothes Campaign and trade unions are key to putting pressure on brands to redesign the fashion industry.

asia.floorwage.org
cleanclothes.org
fairwear.org

Ending slavery and exploitation in India

"Freedom of association is the solution. Everyone knows that, when there is representation and organization of the workers, management is less likely to use illegal means to exploit and harass workers."

Gopinath Kunhithayil Parakuni

India, like many other developing nations, has few workplace trade unions and, as a result, its workers struggle to get their voices heard. But, in October 2016, 1.5 million workers took part in a nationwide strike calling on the Indian government to raise the minimum wage and put in place policies to support the poor.

Cividep India was formed in 2000. It attempts to educate workers about their rights, and campaigns for corporate accountability. Co-founder Gopinath Kunhithayil Parakuni, General Secretary of Cividep in Bangalore, is well versed in the problems workers face and the changes needed to eradicate slavery and exploitation.

'There are about 1,500 factories in Bangalore, with around 500,000 workers, and not a single one of them has signed a collective-bargaining agreement with a trade union. All the big brands are producing here. Workers have a right to organize themselves, but it is not mandatory for companies to recognize trade unions – so this is a loophole. Of course, if you try to organize a union and you are victimized, there are a number of provisions, called unfair labour practices, to protect you, but these workers are from an agricultural background and most of them are women and not very literate, so they are not able to make use of these provisions. They are afraid. It is basically fear with which situations are managed. Industrial relations in the garment industry equates to fear; when workers can't bear the torment,

The Cividep team meets with workers to discuss the barriers that prevent them from negotiating better wages and rights, and eradicating slavery.

Pramita Ray/Cividep

they just walk out. But they need wages, so after a few weeks' or months' rest in their village, they have no choice but to go back to another factory, because they do not have another source of income. But the situation there is the same.'

What are the worst situations reported by garment-factory workers?

Unpaid overtime is a huge issue. If brands improved their buying practices, this would help to reduce overtime. Garment workers often work 16 hours a day and get no rest because they work on Sundays, too. Part of the problem is due to the short turnaround time that the brands want.

However, nowadays we do see that brands prefer long-term relationships – they are consolidating their suppliers. In this way you are more assured of quality and delivery and reduce the risk of subcontracting and slavery.

What are the best ways to help workers?

You need grassroots organizations that have credibility with the workers. This will build trust. You must understand: most social audits are not trusted, because workers think it is all run by management and workers don't open up and tell them what is actually happening. Brands 'parachuting in' and thinking that they can find out what is happening in a day or two just isn't going to work.

There is a huge trust deficit. These are vulnerable people; they need organizations in which they can trust. Building alliances like this takes time and money. I have seen brands and NGOs with the very best intentions actually do some very damaging things.

What the brands must do

'Brands need to be strong,' says Gopinath. 'They have a lot of bargaining power over factory owners and they can make a positive difference. Brands urgently need to bargain on:

- The living wage – low wages are one reason why the workers are so vulnerable. Poverty-level wages really break their back. It is unimaginable: a whole generation of children are being cheated of their development opportunities. They're not going to a good school, they're not wearing good clothes. In my sector, people earn a monthly wage of around 7,000 rupees ($102).

- Freedom of association. Right now, the system is stagnant because of the lack of trade-union strength. How do you capture the violations if there are no factory-level unions in contact with the workforce? There are criminal violations in every factory every day which are not reported because of the vulnerability of the workers. Human rights are routinely violated. You might think this is an exaggeration, but it isn't.

Without these two changes there won't be lasting change. Everything else is just fiddling with stuff.'

For example, they may try to 'train' victims to speak up for themselves, but if you pitch young workers against very powerful, influential factory management, and you claim that your investment is in training the victims, you are wrong – you are actually burdening the victims. You are saying, 'Come on, you have empowered yourselves! Break out of these chains!' But how can they? How can a 15- or 16-year-old girl stand up against management regarding serious labour-law violations? The girls need to have a voice, but that has to be through trade unions. You must have serious engagement with trade unions. You have to make it clear to the management that a workplace without a trade union automatically raises concerns.

cividep.org

Fighting for workers' rights in China

In China, the world's largest producer of clothing, there is little transparency and labour-rights activists are routinely rounded up and imprisoned. So trade-union movements have been difficult to form and campaigning for better practice and improved workers' rights in the country has been incredibly slow.

Hong Kong has a different political and economic system from the rest of China, and provides an international hub, though trade unionists there still face discrimination and there is little protection for workers on the right to collective bargaining. I recently met up with Sophie Chen, from Students and Scholars against Corporate Misbehaviour (SACOM), and Kiki Yeung

of the Hong Kong Confederation of Trade Unions (HKCTU). HKCTU is a trade-union confederation representing 190,000 members and plays a unique role in supporting workers' rights in mainland China.

Kiki and Sophie were in Britain as part of a speaker tour organized by War on Want to promote awareness of human rights violations in China. As we sat sipping cups of Fair Trade coffee, we talked about the urgent changes needed in the fashion industry.

What does modern slavery in the garment industry in China look like?
Sophie: In China's context, modern slavery means forced labour. The basic wage is so meagre that people

"Pretty girls in the factory are always harassed by the male managers. They come on to the girls, ask them into their offices, whisper into their ears, touch them at the waist, arms, neck, buttocks, breasts, bribe them with money and threaten them with losing their jobs to have sex with them."

Liuxia, garment worker in China

Sweater
€ 0,09

4

Iwan Gabovitch under a CC licence

A poster in a metro station exposes the grim reality for Chinese garment workers.

have no choice but to do overtime to boost their salary and make ends meet. Also, workers have no choice because many big fashion brands have a very short lead-time. This means that a factory trying to rush through orders to make the delivery on time will push its employees to do overtime work through the night.

Last month SACOM launched an investigative report showing how factories that are producing garments for fast-fashion brands are pushing workers to do 12-hour days, with only one day off a month. In some extreme cases, factory workers were starting at 7.30am, working through to 2 or 3am, getting a couple of hours' sleep and then starting all over again. We can name these factories and brands.

There are 10 million garment workers in China, compared to 3 million in Bangladesh. Why are your organizations based in Hong Kong rather than mainland China?

Sophie: In Hong Kong there is much more freedom of association, so we have room to do the kind of work we want to. It is really difficult to have demonstrations without obstruction from the government in mainland China. In Hong Kong we have staged at least four or five protests. For example, we walked inside Uniqlo's flagship store to deliver a petition. We couldn't do that in mainland China.

Kiki: We are a trade union organizing Hong Kong workers and we do a lot of work supporting our

Chinese neighbours. In mainland China, the government has strict information censorship. If there is a labour dispute, workers are exploited or mistreated by management, it is very difficult for them to get their message to the outside world and get more support. In these cases, we stage a protest in Hong Kong against the transnational corporation involved. We also link up with other workers' organizations and global trade unions to pressurize the brands and international corporations in order to enhance workers' room for organizing and collective negotiation with the supplier factories.

How does the collusion between government and businesses – which results in oppression and violence – manifest itself?
Kiki: In China, all unions have to be under the umbrella of the All China Federation of Trade Unions (ACFTU), which is not democratically elected by workers – it is just a government department. The ACFTU is the only official trade-union confederation in China and all factory-level trade unions have to be registered by them.

Sophie: It's worth mentioning that China is not the only country where we see this kind of collusion between government and corporations. It is the same in many developing countries. The power of capital and corporations has exceeded the power of government, so the suppression is first from the corporation itself, and then the corporation will leverage the local government to do it a favour. A corporation may pressure the local government or authorities to put in place legislation that is financially favourable to them if, for example, they are going to relocate a factory and they want to avoid paying worker compensation or pensions.

What can consumers do to support Chinese garment workers' rights?
Sophie: The power of corporations overwhelms the power of government. So the consumer needs to target international brands directly. It's very important to have consumers aligned with workers in support of

the truth. We need grassroots organizations monitoring the corporations.

When there is a strike inside a garment factory, it's so important to have consumers' support. For example, in the Global North, where the companies' headquarters are located, consumers should put pressure on the corporations to facilitate collective bargaining between the factory owners and the workers. Or at least let the corporation know that they are being watched.

You were very successful with Uniqlo in Japan – how did media coverage in Japan raise awareness and get Uniqlo to really rethink how it treats workers?
Sophie: SACOM was able to co-operate with labour activists and NGOs based in Japan, including Human Rights Now, LaborNet and Pacific Asia Resource Center. Japan is Uniqlo's biggest market, so it is important for them to maintain a clean and stylish brand image there. We were able to leverage this: what we were exposing was quite shocking and they felt as if they were being seriously attacked. They were forced to at least give an explanation and some reaction in response to us. Support from the Japanese media and the public was crucial.

According to the follow-up investigation, Uniqlo has conducted corrective measures regarding workplace health and safety, including: providing better extractor fans and ventilation (thus reducing the temperature in the factory); improving drainage channels so that there is no chemical sewage on the floor; reducing the risk of electricity leakage onto damp floors; reducing overtime working hours; and revisiting its system of fining workers for punitive matters like making mistakes in their sewing. But it still isn't allowing workers to form their own trade union, so they are still unable to represent themselves.

sacom.hk
en.hkctu.org.hk

HKCTU and SACOM staged a number of protests at UNIQLO's flagship store in Hong Kong between 2014 and 2016, to condemn the brand's negligence on various labour-rights violations in its suppliers. The banners and placards at this protest on 15 July 2015 suggest that UNIQLO was turning a blind eye to the fact that one of its suppliers, Artigas, was ignoring labour laws in China by not paying its workers social insurance and severance pay.

SACOM

MEET
THE
SLAVES.

UNIVERSITY OF WINCHESTER
LIBRARY

HUMAN TRAFFICKING

Across the world, millions of men, women and children are exploited by human traffickers, who take advantage of their poverty and vulnerability to sell them into slavery.

"নারী পাচার করে যারা সমাজের শত্রু তারা"

BEWARE OF TRAFFICKERS!

বাংলাদেশ জাতীয় মহিলা আইনজীবী সমিতি
BANGLADESH NATIONAL WOMEN LAWYERS ASSOCIATION

Miki Alcalde

It is estimated that over a million women and children have been trafficked out of Bangladesh in the past 30 years. Human trafficking is a form of slave trading – it is the buying and selling of human beings. Victims are sold by their family members to people who want to make money out of them, or are abducted and forced into labour. Globally, the trafficking of women, men and children generates $150 billion per year for sex and labour.

'Don't take sweets from strangers' is a lesson many of us were taught as children. Even the very young need to learn that not everyone has their interests at heart. In Bangladesh and other countries with extreme poverty, children and young people are vulnerable to individuals and criminal gangs, perhaps from a nearby village, who circle like vultures, watching out for a family's misfortune, hunger or destitution.

For them, this is a business opportunity: they will lure parents, guardians or the young people themselves with the promise of a well-paid job in the city or overseas. The parents or guardians, who are often illiterate, see this as an opportunity to increase their income, a way out of poverty, and one less mouth to feed. In reality,

This poster has been on the wall of my favourite Fair Trade project in Bangladesh for years. Whenever I saw it, I used to ask myself why, in such a vibrant and happy place, people need to be warned about traffickers. But one day, as I sat in a local tea shop, I heard stories about the 'near escapes' of children and young people and how the poverty around the village was so great that everyone knew of someone who had 'gone missing'. Traffickers and criminal gangs would scour the villages for the most vulnerable but Fair Trade provided an economic shield to protect people.

the 'well-paid job' is usually in domestic servitude, the sex trade, or highly exploitative work. The young person disappears without trace and the family receives meagre or no wages from their slave labour.

In this section we meet those whose lives have been affected by human trafficking.

Safia Minney

Salma Ali sits at her executive glass-topped desk in a tidy, bright, homely office. The inspirational lawyer is surrounded by bookcases which bulge with heavy legal reference books; her walls are peppered with international awards and trophies that celebrate her work.

A helping hand from lawyers in Bangladesh

Bangladesh National Woman Lawyers Association (BNWLA) was formed in 1979 through the committed efforts of Salma Ali and other prominent women lawyers in Bangladesh. They fought for disadvantaged women to get the legal and human rights advice they were entitled to, and helped them to overcome violence and oppression. BNWLA has approximately 1,500 registered women lawyers and highlights and campaigns on key issues such as human trafficking, child and forced marriage, women workers' rights, violence against women and children and domestic violence. It lobbies at local, national and regional level and is increasingly consulted by government departments on relevant issues and changes in the law.

'The women and girls we rescue represent only the tip of the iceberg,' says Salma. 'We repatriate on average 50 Bangladeshi girls a month from India. The border with India is open, so many girls have no idea they are being trafficked across the border. These girls are very young: 14 to 16. Many have been victims of excessive economic insecurity and 30 per cent are garment workers.'

I ask Salma how Western consumers can make a difference. 'They need to understand the seriousness of the situation,' she replies. 'They have to know the facts. Factory owners and fashion buyers should get engaged with the issue of human trafficking. We have comprehensive laws, but they are not enforced in most cases; there should be mechanisms to implement them properly.'

Why is human trafficking such an issue in Bangladesh?

Financial instability makes girls and young women highly vulnerable. They are forced to marry, told they have to take any job and may be abandoned by their parents. When they arrive in the city as a domestic helper or garment worker, most of them are under 18 and have no proper shelter, privacy or support.

Why aren't the traffickers being prosecuted?

They are very organized and keep themselves hidden. Most of the time, even the girls themselves can't identify them. They operate in gangs and trick the girls into coming to the city for a good job, but they usually end up in sex work. Sometimes, traffickers operate outside factory gates – in collusion with the factory managers. We also have a huge problem of corruption in the police.

If garment workers were paid decently and fashion companies planned their production better to ensure continuous employment, would fewer women end up being trafficked?

Yes, I think so. A living wage and regular income would make all the difference. Garment factories could also help to develop protection mechanisms, establish safe shelter facilities to rehabilitate victims of trafficking and train them for decent jobs.

Salma, in her twenties, campaigning for women's rights along with prominent activist Sufia Kamal and others. Salma started her work in women's and children's rights when she and her colleagues realized that women were being put in prison because they had no family to live with or support them: 'We started to represent and defend them, to win back their freedom and help them rebuild their lives.'

Safia Minney

Tulip's story

The girls who are helped by the BNWLA are the lucky ones, caught by honest police officers who contact Salma's organization. Tulip (pictured left) is one of those repatriated by the BNWLA.

'No-one wanted me after my mum's death,' she tells me, 'so I ended up taking a long journey [to India] with others of my age, my uncle and another man from my community. Then the police came and put me in jail for one year.' A grin breaks out on her fine-boned face as she relates her story's happy ending: 'Now I'm back in Bangladesh and going to school and staying at the shelter. I like to stitch and one day I will join a garment factory. I hope to help other girls in future.'

Miki Alcalde

Ms Ali's story

Ms Ali was crying as she spent her bonus trying to call her 17-year-old son, Harit, on her mobile phone from a tiny village in Bangladesh. Four months earlier he had got up one day at 4.30am, pressed 200 taka ($2.50) into his mother's hand and gone out in his T-shirt and jeans, without a bag.

Two months later, Harit called his uncle and said he was working in southern India. Then he hung up and when his mother called back later to speak to him, the line was so bad that she wasn't even sure if it was her son at all. She began to wonder if the person on the other end of the phone was perhaps someone who had enslaved him. Harit hadn't sent any money home, and during their brief call he hadn't asked after his sister. Ms Ali still doesn't know where her son is or when she will see him again.

Escaping the sex trade

> "After I got out of sex work I wanted to help others find freedom and regain the dignity they had once had."
>
> Mina, social worker

In Sonagachi, the red-light district of Kolkata, Mina works as a social worker and social entrepreneur at a Fair Trade business called Freeset (see page 120). She offers the choice of freedom to women who have been trafficked into the sex trade and Freeset provides them with decent employment and support.

As we walk past the line of sex workers waiting for customers, Mina turns to me. 'Don't take photographs; they'll chase you out of Sonagachi,' she warns – and she means it. Mina takes me to meet Parvin, one of the women she helps, a sex worker who recently gave away her baby to a neighbour and is excited to tell us how well the baby is doing. Life in the sex trade is truly living on the edge, and women have to be pragmatic – even to the extent of letting their baby go. Mina and I sit in the bed-sized room where Parvin entertains her clients and where her family of three used to sleep before her husband abandoned her.

There is one window, but this is the smallest room I have ever entered in my life! I measure it with my body: it is narrower than the space between my outstretched arms. Parvin is having a break before she gets busy for the night, and offers us delicious sweet tea and biscuits. We talk about how she came to the sex trade from her village years ago, her life and children, and how difficult it is for her to change her circumstances. We head to Mina's room; it, too, is tiny, squeezed over a stairwell and with just enough space for her to sleep and carry out her administrative work for Freeset.

'I was born in Bangladesh,' Mina tells me when I ask her to relate her story. 'During the war of independence with Pakistan [in 1971], my family escaped to a refugee camp in India. I was 12. I was befriended by a woman who told my family she had good work for me in Kolkata, but she brought me to Sonagachi and sold me to a brothel owner. This was my bad fate.'

What motivated you to help so many women escape from the sex trade?

I had worked in the trade myself – I understand that it is poverty that drives girls to work in the sex trade. I knew that if these girls had proper work, they would get freedom from 'the line'. We help them find ways to educate their children and encourage them to bring their babies to the crèche. When women join Freeset, we give them identity cards so they can prove they are in dignified work.

How many women work in Sonagachi?

There are 10,000 girls and young women working in the sex trade here. However, they don't earn as much money as they did before; they have to go out and find work in hotels or even travel to Mumbai under a contract for two or three months. My dream is to bring good jobs in businesses like Freeset to 20,000 women. We started with only 20 women; now we have about 250. So far I have helped about 300 to 400 women to leave the sex trade and join freedom businesses like Sari Bari, Kolkata Arts, Freeset, Loyal and Dhulian.

Safia Minney

Mina shows me her family album and we stumble across her picture as a young girl.

Anandi's story

"I never thought I'd have the opportunity to be trained and work in textiles."

Anandi, Freeset employee

A religious festival is taking place as Anandi leads Mina and me to her home village. We make our way through the throngs to the top of the hill where her house sits, past the crowds celebrating Durga Puja with their red powder-painted faces. The deity around whom they have been dancing will be plunged into the river at dawn.

Anandi, who has a speech impediment, uses sharp exclamations and gesticulations to tell us how excited she is to be introducing us to her mother, and to be sharing the story of her journey back to her village from Sonagachi in Kolkata and how she found her new job at Freeset Fabrics.

At her home, we settle around a pot of tea and talk loudly so as to hear ourselves above the partying crowd. It is best to talk at home, away from the gossips, says Anandi's mother – even though the whole village knows the sad reality of life for the very poor, for whom sex work in Kolkata's infamous red-light district may be the only route to survival.

Anandi managed to escape from the sex trade. Mina says she spotted her 'in "the line" in Sonagachi, and I found out she was from here. I told her, "You could be free! You could either work with us in Kolkata at Freeset, or at our handloom weaving business in your village. You could live with your mother again."

Anandi had arrived in Kolkata at the age of 15 with Prakash, the criminal who trafficked her. Selling Anandi into the sex trade paid for her father's operation and for the marriage of her niece. 'I was badly beaten by Prakash,' she says, 'and then by the madam, who used to hit my face so much it swelled up. Whenever I asked for money from her, she used to kick me. "Where is the money?" she used to say. It's good that I have left that place and we are safe and happy here. The brothel madam was not good; her face was always miserable.'

Anandi's mother chips in: 'When my daughter went to Kolkata I was very worried about her and that I was allowing her to go. What should I do? What would happen to her? I am her mother, only I understand my pain. I carried her in my womb, I brought her up. She's a girl with a speech problem. If I die, what will become of her?'

When I ask if she was sent money regularly, Anandi's mother says that this was not the case, though she says that during Puja her daughter used to bring her new clothes. 'I used to say to her that clothing is very costly – it's better that you give me money so I can spend it on food. Whatever little money Anandi sent I used to buy rice and dal – I needed to take care of all the family. I worried about the future and what would become of her when I died. I bought a piece of land in the field and a small house to provide for her.'

For Anandi, working at the factory, which runs on Fair Trade principles, is a dream come true. 'I really enjoy the respect and dignity of working at Freeset,' she explains. 'I never thought I'd have the opportunity to be trained and work in textiles.'

Miki Alcaide

Anandi escaped the sex trade in Kolkata to find Fair Trade work back at her village.

BONDED LABOUR

"Bonded labour exists because of the persistence of poverty… large groups of people vulnerable to exploitation, and the existence of people who are prepared to exploit the desperation of others."

antislavery.org

Aloysius Arockiam, the director of SAVE.

Miki Alcalde

Bonded labour is the least known yet most widespread form of slavery in the world. It is illegal, yet governments are rarely willing to enforce the law or punish those who profit from the exploitation of weak and vulnerable people. A person becomes a bonded labourer when they are made to work in repayment for a loan. However, the value of their work invariably exceeds the original sum of money borrowed.

This form of modern slavery flourishes in agriculture, brick kilns, mills and factories all over the world, including in the textile mills of southern India that feed the fashion industry. It is often found in mills and factories operating the form of child labour known in India as Sumangali.

In order to find out more about the Sumangali scheme, I went to talk to Aloysius Arockiam, who works for Social Awareness and Voluntary Education (SAVE), a non-governmental organization that exposes the working and living conditions of textile and garment workers in Tirupur, India's knit capital.

What is the Sumangali scheme and how does it enslave girls and young women?
The scheme started in the late 1980s. It offers parents, usually from poor and low-caste families, the chance to sign up their daughters for a three-year contract working in a factory. Often the girls are as young as 14. Once they are recruited, they are sent to a mill many hundreds of kilometres away, so as to keep them far from their families. They are supposed to be housed and fed and receive a lump sum of around 60,000 rupees [$900] after three years. This money helps them to pay for a dowry and to get married.

The girls have to live in a hostel and all their labour and human rights are violated: long hours, no freedom, no access to the outside world, cruel treatment. They are forced to work 12 to 16 hours a day, they are not allowed to leave the factory and are often sacked mid-term to save the employer from paying them at all. Their compensation when they leave, if it is actually paid, is a fraction of the minimum wage they are entitled to. Sumangali is illegal by Indian law. The psychological and physical damage done to these victims impairs them for life.

"These are young women, aged 16-21. They only eat a little food and have no rest. Their bodies become very weak after a couple of years working like this so ultimately, when they get married, their health is ruined."

Aloysius Arockiam, director, SAVE

I read a newspaper article about a young girl who couldn't bear it any more and threw herself from the window of her dormitory...
The pressure just gets too much.
Yes, it is shocking; 200 girls have committed suicide in the last two years in similar circumstances. Once they are in the factory, the gates are locked and they can't get out. They are not even allowed to call home. The youngsters don't want to upset their parents, but they want to be released. Threatening to jump out of a window or overdose on medicine seems to be the only way of trying to get sympathy from their parents.

I witnessed a particularly sad case recently. A girl asked again and again if she could be let free and return home. Eventually, her brother travelled the 200 kilometres to get her. He arrived late at night and had to stay in a hostel. By the morning, the girl had given up hope and killed herself. The factories cover up all these deaths by saying that the girls have fallen in love with a boy, that they have disgraced themselves and out of shame have killed themselves. It is all a lie.

How many girls are working under the Sumangali scheme?
There are about 200,000 girls trapped in this scheme, in almost all the 2,200 mills in Tamil Nadu, south India. This is a deep-rooted problem in the spinning and textile sector. We rescued about 2,800 girls last year.

What can the fashion industry do to make sure it is not supporting this terrible situation?
If buyers see dormitories attached to a mill, they should be suspicious and investigate, even if the presence of the Sumangali scheme is denied. Audits should be done with local NGOs and trade unions. They must check beyond the first tier of their supply chain: if they don't do this, how can they have any control over who is making clothes for them?

When they place an order with a factory, they should look at whether it has the capacity to deliver from their own production unit. If not, buyers need to find out who the factory will subcontract to and investigate them, too. Embroidery and sewing on sequins happens in people's homes, where poor pay and child labour is rife; buyers need to find out when and where this is happening and follow up. Brands need to work together on this.

Factories can do a lot to help train young women in life skills, literacy, numeracy and assembly work [sewing a sleeve onto the body of a garment]. I would like to see the women trained to make a whole garment, so they can start their own tailoring business after they return to their villages and start a family.

Aloysius introduced me to Varsha, now 15 years old, who has worked in a mill where many of her co-workers were part of the Sumangali scheme. Her story, on page 69, gives a glimpse of life as a child working in a big textile mill.

THE NEW
INDIAN EXPRESS

COIMBATORE TUESDAY 13 NOVEMBER 2012

12 BROKERS HELD

o Minor AP, K'taka Girls Rescued in Tirupur

press News Service

irupur: Ten minor girls, ought here by brokers m Andhra Pradesh and rnataka, were rescued on nday.

Police said their rescue fol- ved Oasis India, a Banga- e-based NGO, getting a -off on these girls being ken by a group to some er place under suspicious cumstances. The girls and brokers with them belong places near the Karnataka-

Andhra Pradesh border.

About 10 volunteers of the NGO followed this group, along with the girls, when they boarded a train from Bangalore on Sunday night. When they got down at Tiru- pur railway station on Mon- day, the volunteers informed the Tirupur North police who arrested the 12 brokers and rescued the girls.

As the brokers could not properly answer the ques- tions or explain why the mi- nor girls were brought to

Tirupur, the police strongly suspect that they were brought to the city as bonded labourers. All the 12 brokers with the girls were taken into police custody for further questioning and investiga- tion. The rescued girls have been sent to a home run by Mariyalaya, a local NGO.

Police sources said a joint meeting of police, a medical team and Child Welfare Com- mittee would be conducted on Thursday to discuss fur- ther course of action.

HOME AWAY FROM HOME: The minor girls from Andhra and Karnataka being taken to a rescue home in Tirupur | V Sakthi

---

COIMBATORE

THE HINDU • TUESDAY, OCTOBER 16, 2012

77 bonded labourers rescued from Erode textile mill

Staff Reporter

ERODE: Officials in the district rescued 77 persons, including children, who were allegedly forced into bonded labour at a private yarn processing mill in Erode on Monday.

Mayor Mallika Paramasi- vam, who received informa- tion from the people living in Arumugam Street in Karun- galpalayam area about the bonded labourers, alerted po- lice and revenue officials.

A team of police personnel monitored the mill for the past 10 days and the prelimi- nary investigations revealed that persons were forced into

bonded labour at the mill.

A team of officials led by the Mayor conducted a sur- prise check at the mill on Monday afternoon and res- cued 77 bonded labourers. The labourers included more than 30 children.

Official sources said the la- bourers were brought to the mill from different parts of Dharmapuri and Krishnagiri districts. Many labourers claimed that they were paid a sum of Rs. 10,000 as advance to work at the mill. It had been several months since they were allowed to visit their home. "We were forced to work in the unit as there

was no employment opportu- nities in our area, " said the labourers from Marandahalli in Dharmapuri district.

Collector V.K. Shanmugam and District Revenue Officer S. Ganesh also rushed to the spot and directed the author- ities to conduct a detail probe. "A case will be registered against the management of the mill and a detailed inves- tigation launched. In the pre- liminary enquiry, we found the mill did not have proper approval from the author- ities," he said. Doctors from the GH have been asked to examine the children to de- termine their age.

THE NEW INDIAN EXPRESS
COIMBATORE WEDNESDAY 17 OCTOBER 2012

61 MORE CHILDREN RESCUED

Express News Service

Erode: Sixty-one more child labourers, who were spotted with an industrial unit holder at Mannathampalayam, 30 kilometres away from here, were rescued on Tuesday. The Revenue officials had, on Monday, saved 27 children from a spinning mill near here.

The kids were spotted at the *mandapam* of Kulavilak- ku Amman Temple in Nanjai Kalamangalam village on Erode-Karur Road by Depu- ty Tahsildar Gunasekaran and Revenue Inspector Bu- vaneswaran, who were on an official visit to the village.

When confronted, unitholder Suresh claimed that he was sending the chil- dren back home fearing ac- tion against his unit in the wake of crackdown against units employing children.

However, VAOs S Amsaraj and V Gurusev of nearby vil- lages, after an inquiry said the children were working at Dhanalakshmi spinning mill in Solar and were brought there in buses. They also said that inquiry revealed that 12 boys and 10 girls were below 14 and seven boys and 32 girls below 17. The children are currently kept in Jeeva Government Home for Chil- dren near RTO office and will be taken to the GH on Wednesday, they added.

However, Suresh rebutted officials' claim that he owned the unlicensed mill at Ra- jagopal Thottam, from where 27 kids were rescued on Monday. **MORE: P3**

EW INDIAN EXPRESS
BATORE FRIDAY 13 JULY 2012

Raid on Mills After Activists Free 'Sumangali' Workers

Express News Service

lem: After activists of e AITUC and Tirupur ople's Forum (TPF) freed o sisters bonded under e Sumangali scheme om the Pallipalayam inning Mills at Seelani- npatti, the Department Labour and Revenue, on ursday, jointly raided ills in the area that prac- se the system.

Inspector of Labour K nkatesan, Inspector of ctories H A Rahman and lem RDO Prasanna Ra- samy led the raid. Their dings confirm the prac- e in the mills. However, action can be taken be- se of a pending court

few of their woes. Apart from harsh working condi- tions, the girls face sexual harassment from male col- leagues and the owners. The employment contract is for four years at a month- ly wage of ₹2,500, at the end of which the girls are sent home with a terminal benefit of ₹45,000.

However, the mills usu- ally find excuses to settle for lower terminal benefits, says Vimalan, an activist representing AITUC.

Vimalan said TPF had received information about two girls, Sathya and Nithya (sisters from Villupuram), wanting to be freed of ha- rassment at the Pallipa- layam Spinning Mills. The

THE TIMES OF INDIA, COIMBATORE •
FRIDAY, JULY 13, 2012

Raid at Salem mill reveals girls employed as bonded labour

A M Shudhagar

Miki Alcalde

Varsha's story

"There were 500 children my age working in that spinning mill... the men talked roughly to us. I became frightened."

Varsha, garment worker

Varsha's pretty smile glows as she welcomes me into her home. She tells me that she has been cooking chicken for her family's lunch; she is not unhappy to be interrupted. The 15-year-old lives in a small, two-roomed, government-built house: her uncle's family lives in one room and Varsha lives in the other with her mother, father and grandmother.

Like many Dalit farming families in the area, they are the worst off in their community and are discriminated against at every turn. Many still live with the stigma of untouchability.

Varsha takes me to her family's room, their home. I compliment her on its spaciousness and the soft aquamarine painted walls. Then we sit down and she tells me her story.

'I started working at the age of 12 at a spinning mill, cleaning sticks out of the cotton. I worked from 6am until 2pm, which was one of the three shifts at the mill. After work, I would come home and relax. I didn't think of going to school.

'I remember there were about 50 girls living in a dormitory which was part of the mill. They worked the night shift but, as I lived locally, I did a day shift.

'The girls came from the villages around Tamil Nadu. Many of them were young, between 10 and 14 years old. After three years working at the mill they get a lump sum of 80,000 rupees [$1,200] and that gives them enough money to pay for their marriage. They also get a little "pocket money", like 500 rupees a month, and free meals and accommodation. That's how they survive. There were 500 children my age working in that spinning mill. I was with my friends and sometimes we would play music and play a little – that was great!

'After about a year I couldn't stay at the mill any longer because the noise became too much for me and the men talked roughly to us. I became frightened. But I was lucky to be free and I could leave.'

CHILD LABOUR

The term 'child labour' is often defined as work that deprives children of their childhood, their potential and their dignity, and that is harmful to their physical and mental development.

Rabeya and Razia hold up a Fair Trade T-shirt.

Child labour deprives children of the opportunity to attend school or the chance to play. It perpetuates poverty across generations by keeping poor children out of school and limiting their prospects for upward social mobility. In its most extreme forms, it involves children being enslaved, separated from their family, exposed to serious danger and left to fend for themselves.

The reasons that child labour persists are manifold. In rural areas, a lack of job opportunities for adults can result in parents having little option but to allow their children to work; in urban areas, though parents may have jobs, the low wages they are paid are insufficient to meet their family's needs, and children are sent to work to supplement the household income. It is estimated that, if adults were paid a fair living wage, child labour would decrease by a third.

Tackling child labour within the global fashion industry relies on brands having a much better overview of every link in their supply chain. Children are often 'employed' at the very bottom of the supply chain, where they are untraceable and invisible.

News of forced child labour in the cotton fields of Uzbekistan and of Syrian refugee children found in Turkish garment factories has forced major brands to engage more seriously with their supply chains. Yet children are still chosen as tailors and helpers in garment factories and for sequin and embellishment tasks in small workshops throughout Asia – they have small hands, they are obedient, and their wages are lower than adults' pay.

In Bangladesh, children between the age of 16 and 18 are allowed to work in a garment factory, but legally they can only work for five hours, not eight hours, and they can work the day shift not the night shift.

With this in mind, I went to meet some of the children who work in the garment industry in Dhaka, Bangladesh, a city known as the garment-producing capital of the world.

Mukta

Mukta is 15 years old and has worked at a knitwear company in the capital since she was 12.

'When I was six, I came to Dhaka with my brother. We lived with my cousin and I studied until I was 12. But my parents became unwell, so I had no choice but to start working. I went to the factory, where my brother was already working. When I started work the wages were very small, only 1,400 taka ($17) per month. Now I earn 6,250 taka ($79) per month; there is no overtime in our factory.

'We originally come from Mymensingh. I really miss my parents; we only see them about three times a year.'

Miki Alcalde

Miki Alcalde

Monzur

Fifteen-year-old Monzur has been working at a knitwear factory for a year. He is a quality checker: 'Sometimes we have to stop the whole shipment if we have a quality problem,' he tells me.

His basic salary is 3,000 taka ($38) per month, which goes up to 5,000 taka ($63) per month with overtime. 'My family were forced to buy some land. They had to sell everything, including all our cows and goats; they also had to borrow money. In order to pay the loan, a friend advised my father and me to go to Dhaka to find work. I tried to go to school, but the financial pressure got too great, so my father said I had to start working at the garment factory to earn money.

'One day, I want to make enough money to buy a tractor for agricultural work, so my father and I can go back to our village and work together.'

Jahanara

Jahanara is 14 years old. She started working as a tailor at the age of 13. For the past month, she has worked for the same knitwear company as Monzur. In the photo, she is holding some Japanese labels. 'I chose this factory because it's very close to my house,' she says. 'There are 300-400 people that work there. About half of the workers are 14 years old or younger.'

Jahanara's basic salary is 5,200 taka ($66) per month; with overtime she earns 7,000 ($89). As a tailor, she earns well compared to helpers and finishers, who receive much less.

Jahanara took out a loan for a tea shop that her brother runs and a metal shop next door that her father runs. Most of the household income is from her job and most of her earnings are being used to repay the loans for the shops.

Rajib

Rajib is 16 years old and works as a sewing helper. He does overtime every day, which means he works 13 hours a day. His basic salary is 3,500 taka ($44) per month, but with overtime it is 5,500 ($70).

'I was a student, but my family suddenly faced hardship and I had to start working. My father was ill; he had a tumour. I had to earn money and help my father to get well again. He now owns a small shop in Dhaka.

'My dream is to earn enough money in the garment factory to go back to my village and open my own shop selling party decorations.'

Almost all of the teenage garment workers I met were working overtime like adults, which is not allowed.

Miki Alcalde

Miki Alcalde

Arifa

Arifa is 15 and works at a knitwear factory, earning 5,500 taka ($70) per month. 'My family took loans, and my parents are old. They need medical care and there are other regular family expenses that my salary contributes towards.'

Miki Alcalde

Sisters Rabeya and Razia

Rabeya is 14 and works in a factory that has 100 workers – half of whom are children like her. She is a helper and is very excited because her manager has promised that next month she will be promoted to a tailor. She earns 4,000 taka ($50) per month and works eight hours a day. Her mother is ill and can't work; her father earns just 3,000 taka ($38) per month as a rickshaw puller. Her older sister Razia, who is 16 and a screen printer, has been working in the garment industry since she was 11 and now earns 6,700 taka ($85) per month.

'The main problem is work pressure,' says Rabeya. 'Children can't operate the heavy machinery or make the targets we are set. When we try to tell the factory managers that we can't manage the work, they just say: "Others can do it – you also have to do it!" This makes us cry and feel very bad. We feel like a failure and inadequate. Some children are bigger and have greater strength than the smaller children.

'Sometimes the managers fire the children because they can't do the work. Or, if children are absent for a day or two, they get fired with no pay or compensation. My dream is to start a tailoring shop with my older sister [pictured here], who is also a garment worker. If I could earn more money, perhaps I could save up to do this.'

INTIMIDATION AND SEXUAL HARASSMENT

Fear silences many women in the workplace – and their male bosses exploit their position through inappropriate physical contact, sexual advances and lewd language.

Miki Alcalde

Deepa says she was fired, when she was six months' pregnant, after someone planted a roll of cellotape in her water-bottle bag. They claimed she stole it and she was fired on the spot. 'I think it's also so unfair that men get tea breaks and women do not,' she adds.

The fashion industry can offer women with limited skills and literacy the opportunity to train, earn a decent wage and improve their own and their family's lives. Across the world, rural development is largely neglected, so there are few job opportunities in their home villages. Women have no choice but to migrate to the cities in the hope of finding decent work. What awaits them is often hugely challenging – poor accommodation, intimidation and sexual harassment in the workplace.

I found that sexual harassment takes many forms. Women suffer sexual harassment where they work and where they live, through sexually charged language, physical contact and advances, and the negotiation for job security in return for sexual favours. Girls and women who do not accept the sexual advances of their boss find they have no choice but to leave the workplace – and any job security, promotion or maternity rights are lost. Such mistreatment must stop. Only when women no longer experience fear in the workplace will they have a voice and an equal chance of promotion and decent wages. Fashion brands can help tackle the problem by talking directly with women workers, supporting their committees, punishing intimidation and sexual harassment and promoting women's rights.

Yet better business practice and long-term planning within the fashion industry, along with brand and consumer awareness and pressure, could give women the chance of decent pay and working conditions, and help in the development of their countries. Women are the greatest resource of nations, yet their unequal social status as second-class citizens is undermining social equity, development and the future of many communities and economies in the Global South.

Over the past 25 years, I have set up Fair Trade supply chains that put women's rights and the environment at the centre of the business and all its operations. Even in the most chauvinistic societies, Fair Trade women's groups have proven that women can be leaders in management and promote opportunities for young women that follow and are inspired by them. We need to take this model from the Fair Trade movement and bring it into mainstream fashion supply chains.

Miki Alcalde

'Women are exploited as they are totally unaware of their rights,' says Elizabeth Khumallambam.

Organizing migrant women in the community

I meet Elizabeth Khumallambam in Gurgaon, near Delhi. She is senior co-ordinator of Nari Shakti Manch, which campaigns and supports women migrant workers whose rights are violated. 'We organize migrant women in the community and work at a political, economic and social level to address the problems they face,' Elizabeth tells me. 'They are exploited as they are totally unaware of their rights. In the garment industry, they are badly paid and not given regular work. In their communities they are forced to buy groceries at a shop in the building where they rent a room at exorbitant prices. If they try to buy from cheaper shops, they get in trouble.'

What other kinds of problems do they experience?
There is a lot of sexual harassment and innuendo at work. Male supervisors will get uncomfortably close to a woman sewing and say 'is the hole big enough? Put the thread inside the hole very carefully'. Men treat women like they are Bollywood actresses – making lewd comments about wearing more modern and colourful clothes. This is a shock to innocent village women. Male supervisors also make advances to their female employees: 'Come out with me for lunch or dinner – then you will get a good salary and your job will be safe.' These women are married and are put in a very difficult situation as their jobs are at risk if they say no. Sexual harassment is one of the main reasons women give for leaving their job.

Has the situation improved since the Sexual Harassment of Women at Workplace Act 2013 was passed?
We are helping women understand what is acceptable behaviour and what is not. For example, a tap on the shoulder is okay, but for a man to touch a woman's stomach is not. Scolding and using abusive language is very common in the garment industry. Women get used to language around them like 'motherfucker' and 'sisterfucker'. This is not acceptable.

Does this kind of language inhibit women's ability to speak up for their rights?
Women who ask too many questions or request clarifications are told to leave. They need to fight this collectively. Men use the power of intimidation. They say, if you want to work here, it's on our terms.

Why don't more women stand up for each other in the workplace?
If a woman who has been working in the garment industry for 15 years knows her rights and goes to meetings, she is treated as a troublemaker by management and the newer women worry that talking to her will cost them their jobs.

What can the brands do to protect their workers?
We need brands and buyers to re-check that factories are doing what they are supposed to. The government set the minimum wage in November 2015, but we know that at least 50 per cent of women are not getting it. Brands need to sign fair contracts with the factory and have direct interaction with women workers.

Most factories have internal workers' committees on paper, but in reality the workers know nothing about them. Some companies are starting awareness-raising programmes on sexual harassment and we see this as a way we can help, by training them to treat men and women equally. Also, we have approached the government about women's safety and security in the workplace.

Women moving from one job to another have no continuous employment and lose their rights; they never get promotion and struggle with low pay and discrimination. Consumers can ask questions, but the women workers can't. They are not physically bonded, but they are bonded in a psychological sense. Intimidation keeps them poor and struggling.

Seema's story

Miki Alcalde

"Why are women not looked at the same way as men? ... I want the same status, but I am not treated equally."

Seema, garment worker

A lot of problems are due to the line managers: they try to find fault with our work. They told me, 'If you start a relationship with me, I will overlook your mistakes.' When I bent down to pick something up, they would make lewd comments: 'I can see your body parts.' They offered me money to have sexual relations with them.

I feel humiliated, I feel ashamed to be a woman. I have children, I need to work. I wish I didn't have to come to Delhi, but I have no choice. I work in a small factory now, as I was denied work with larger fashion factories because I publicly reported the harassment and was blacklisted from larger factories.

I am in a desperate situation; my husband earns 15,000 rupees ($220) a month as a driver. I don't

I am 32 years old and have two sons, aged 14 and 18. I started working in the garment industry seven years ago. I began in leather, cutting threads. When I made a mistake, my line manager stabbed me in the thigh with his pencil until it bled. I slapped him to defend myself, so they fired me. They tore up the paper which showed how many days I had worked and refused to pay me. I got a new job doing other piece-rate work, and now I am working as a tailor.

Miki Alcalde

have enough to eat; I have a big bill at the food-ration shop in my apartment block and I am obliged to buy provisions from there. Also, my husband left me and married another woman. For the last three months I have been unable to send money home for my sons, 24 hours away by train in Jacar. Why are women not looked at the same way as men? I come out of the house and I want the same status, but I am not treated equally. Don't say that it is wrong for women to work. I have two children and I cannot pay my bills. I cannot raise my children without a job. Don't be prejudiced against women, give us equality! I need a job with overtime for 12,000 rupees ($180) a month to survive.

FORCED AND EXCESSIVE LABOUR

Workers are often trapped by poverty wages with little chance to negotiate their terms of employment. Freedom of association and a living wage would eradicate this form of modern slavery.

Miki Alcalde

Latifa walks me though the slums in Dhaka where she lives. She wants to show me that on slave wages – even with forced and excessive overtime – garment workers cannot afford a decent place to live or decent food to eat.

The majority of garment workers in Bangladesh are victims of forced labour, though it is called 'excessive' overtime. Forced labour is a form of modern slavery. Many people work between 60 and 77 hours a week with no guarantee of a day off. Less than half of the workers have a written contract, and few of those who do actually understand its content, due to a low level of literacy. It is estimated that between 30 and 40 per cent of workers in Bangladesh do not earn the minimum wage, let alone a living wage.

Overtime is mostly involuntary (and unpaid in some cases); refusal to work overtime carries with it the threat of losing your job, which is difficult to face for people living hand to mouth. Wages are so low that workers are trapped by the necessity of working extra hours just to feed themselves and their families. Freedom of association would help these workers negotiate better wages and work conditions and protect them from becoming victims of forced labour.

On a cool summer's night, cooking smells and chatter fill the air. This multistorey slum dwelling in Tejgaon, Dhaka, is home to 100,000 people and 25 garment factories that fill the pockets of local landlords and international businesspeople. I have come here to find out more about the conditions of the people who make our clothes.

Latifa is keen to show me her home. She takes my hand; she has soft hands for someone who works so hard. Her grip becomes firmer as she leads me through the typically dangerous slums that I have become accustomed to over the two decades of learning about workers in our fashion industry. We pick our route along a planked pathway that is raised above a stinking pond. There are two sets of pipes running alongside the pathway, one for water and one for gas, and large holes and protruding bits of metal scaffolding that slow us down in the dark. This is not a place to bring up children; most parents leave them with their grandparents in the village and see them only once or twice a year.

UNIVERSITY OF WINCHESTER LIBRARY

Miki Alcalde

Latifa's story

Latifa is 28 and works as a tailor. Her basic monthly salary is 7,000 taka ($89). With overtime, she earns 9,500 taka ($121) per month. Latifa is only allowed to take one or two days off each month.

'I came to Dhaka from Mymensingh over 20 years ago,' she tells me. 'I live here with my husband. We have a 14-year-old son who lives with my mother in the village. I rarely see him.'

I ask Latifa to show me photos of her family, but she only has an old photo of her son as a baby. 'I wish that I could earn enough to be part of my son's life,' she says. 'And that I could regularly take one day off each week. That way, I would have some chance of seeing him.

'Through protests, the conditions are improving bit by bit and the manager's behaviour is better. I have diabetes. I really need a five-minute tea break twice a day. I arrive at the factory at 7.55am and lunch is at 1.30pm. So if I could eat something like a biscuit or fruit and drink a little water at 10am that would really help my body. Another five-minute break at 5pm, as I only finish work at 8pm, would make all the difference to me. It's inhumane to work for such long hours. Customers do not know how hard we work and how the management treat us and how low our wages are. Please tell them!'

Miki Alcalde

Nazma's story

The single-room homes of garment workers in Dhaka, Bangladesh, are typical of the slums that house the four million workers who make the clothes for our high-street brands.

I enter the simple, one-room home of Nazma. She is 27 years old and originally from a village called Narsindghi which is about two hours from Dhaka by public transport.

Nazma shares her single-roomed home with her husband, who works in film. There are stainless steel pots and clothes tidy and clean, all perfectly folded. The exposed concrete walls are an economy rather than fashionable; there are sheets of corrugated iron from 2.5 metres up where they seem to have run out of concrete. I notice a rat run up the wall and wiggle its

bottom through the gap between the wall and the corrugated iron roof.

Nazma works as a tailor. She works 11 hours a day, seven days a week. She tells me she has two daughters, aged 12 and 8 years, who live in Narsindghi. She sees her children twice a year during the Eid holidays; this is her only free time.

'We cannot say no... we are forced to work overtime."

Afzal (right), 26, tailor.

Miki Alcalde

Kausar (left) is 24 and has been a quality inspector at a garment factory for four years. He works 77 hours a week and gets just two days off a month.

'Even in an emergency, if a family member is very sick, it is very difficult to get a day off even if we plead.' He looks down at his hands wearily, remembering when he desperately wanted to help a family member back in his village, but couldn't in case he lost the job that fed his family back home. 'We have no choice. It is regular practice. We want to ask for one day's holiday each week.

'We don't want this life.'

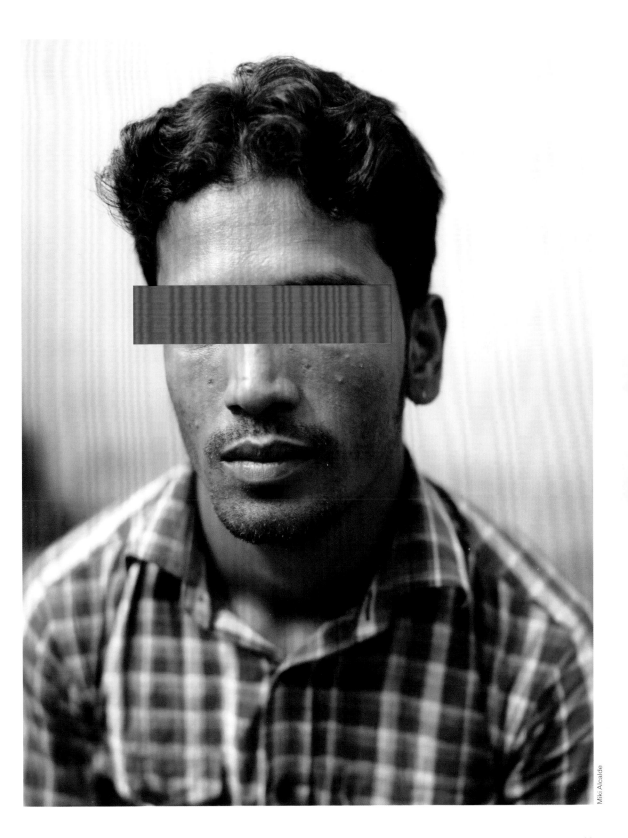

Miki Alcalde

NOW YOU

Latifa in Bangladesh:

I'm legally entitled to a tea break twice a day... it would make such a difference if I could take this and eat a biscuit or drink a juice as I have diabetes.

Profit made by the brand she works for: $2.7 million

Vatey in Cambodia:

My husband was fired from his job for standing up for the rights of other garment workers. Now he has been blacklisted and only gets low-paid work.

Profit made by the brand she works for: $12.5 million

Seema in India:

My line manager made sexual advances and after two years I couldn't stand it any more and left, losing all my benefits.

Profit made by the brand she works for: $7.5 million

Fighting for worker empowerment in Cambodia

"Brands and consumers should pay more for their clothes; we cannot feed our families on these low prices. Tell the brands and customers back home that they can make a huge difference to our lives."

Mr Kim, garment worker

It is five o'clock in the morning and the sun isn't even up when I am collected by Vong Vuthi (pictured top right), Co-ordinator of the Coalition of Cambodian Apparel Workers Democratic Union, the CCAWDU. My eyes are swollen due to lack of sleep. When we stop to refuel, the always good-tempered Miki, our photographer and filmmaker, says he needs coffee. We are on the last leg of three weeks of non-stop research and reporting.

We leave the motorway near the outskirts of Phnom Penh and drive along the bustling roads of the garment-factory district. Women vendors are starting to set up their stands in the streets, putting out their baskets of vegetables, hanging up fresh fish and meat. There are flower sellers trading delicate and colourful blossoms of all kinds. It looks like paradise...

Everything seems peaceful, but in this part of Cambodia's capital city there have recently been violent clashes between riot police and garment workers protesting for their rights. The CCAWDU is leading the campaign for the minimum wage to be raised by 30 per cent, from 565,000 riel ($140) to 714,000 riel ($177) per month. It is also demanding the abolition of illegal short-term contracts and an end to the unlawful firing of unionized workers.

The average Cambodian garment worker toils for 72 hours a week, due to low wages and forced overtime. Many garment factories are not registered with the government and pay their workers just 403,000 riel ($100) a month, well below the current minimum wage. These illegal factories are increasingly being given subcontracts by tier-one suppliers. Their workers receive poor pay, are put onto illegal three-month contracts (even if they have been employed there for years), and have no access to paid holiday, sick leave or maternity leave. Cambodian garment workers are increasingly left vulnerable, hungry and facing economic hardship.

Safia Minney

Miki Alcalde

Mr Kim tells me more about life working in the fashion industry in Cambodia. The thirty-something is proudly wearing a smart polo shirt with the CCAWDU logo embroidered on his breast. 'There are 1,800 workers at my factory; 1,300 of us are members of the union. I have worked in the factory for nine years, and becoming a union member meant I got a long-term contract. I earn the government minimum wage of $140 per month. I do a 10-hour shift and get one day off a week, but my rent is $250 per month for my family of four. My wife gave up her factory job last month to set up a fruit stall outside the factory, to earn more. We cannot survive on $140 per person per month. If brands managed their production better and gave continuous orders, and if they kept a close eye on whether the orders were being subcontracted to illegal factories, where pay and conditions are worse, that would help all Cambodian garment-factory workers.'

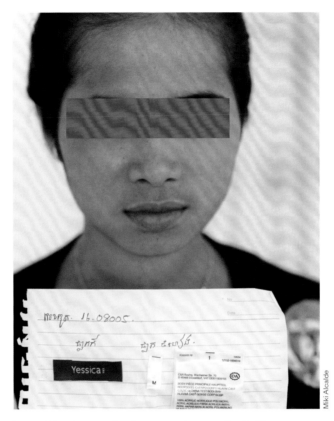

Miki Alcalde

Lita is 21 and earns $170 per month as a tailor in Phnom Penh. 'I joined the union because I wanted job security beyond a short-term contract; if I work here for more than two years, the company is legally obliged to give me a long-term, permanent contract.

'The company should take care of the health of its workers. There are no fans and sometimes it's 31°C and I'm having to work without water. When there is an inspection, staff put water and fans in the factory, but they are taken away after a few days.'

A guard outside a factory in Phnom Penh gives us a steely look
as we watch female garment workers arrive for their shift.

Miki Alcalde

Miki Alcalde

The CCAWDU is demanding better pay and conditions for garment workers in factories such as the one above, including:

- An increase in the monthly minimum wage from $140 to $177
- Constant, reliable and stable orders from buyers
- The supply of drinking water for workers
- A long-term contract for workers after two years in a factory.

SOCIAL INNOVATION & TECHNICAL SOLUTIONS

Progress towards a slave-free, healthy, sustainable world is being shaped by innovative, ethical business tools and technological advances.

Miki Alcalde

As I travelled through Bangladesh and India, I realized the incredible opportunity for transparency that has arisen thanks to the spread of smartphones and apps, which are now being used by the poor and vulnerable to anonymously report to trade unions unsafe work conditions, unpaid salaries and abuse. Information is king, but how can we help accelerate this process?

In 2006, I received a letter from Hilde and Klaus Schwab, founders of the World Economic Forum, asking whether I would accept an award and join their network of the world's outstanding social entrepreneurs. There was just one problem: I had no idea what a social entrepreneur was. I – like many people from diverse backgrounds and professions – was just getting on with it, applying my experience, skills and passion to try to solve a variety of social and environmental problems by founding and running a Fair Trade business.

A decade on, there is huge body of academic research, business theory and indicators on the subject, and no leading business school is complete without a course in social enterprise. Social innovation is not charity. It uses the tools of business, enterprise and market demand to create a sustainable, scalable model. Social businesses are often disruptors in their field, setting agendas and creating social and environmental change by building long-term relationships with their customers and suppliers. They are active in Fair Trade, renewable energy, waste management, recycling, ethical finance, repurposing buildings, and innovating to create new fibres, fabrics and supply chains. The benefits of organic agriculture are being spread by reducing water consumption with modern drip irrigation and providing strong farmer networks, and better organic insecticides like neem. Mobile phones are being used to give farmers better market access and information on prices as they change daily. There has never been a more interesting and critical time to design solutions for a slave-free, healthy, sustainable world.

In this chapter we learn how social innovation is shaping the fashion industry, helping to promote transparency and sustainable livelihoods, and deliver social impact for those most in need, particularly women in rural areas. We look at just a few of the hundreds of thousands of social businesses, organizations and initiatives tackling the root causes of poverty, which makes people vulnerable to traffickers. With few job opportunities and difficulty providing food for themselves or their families, people become easy targets for exploitation by the mills and the factories; many earn less than the minimum wage and work excessive overtime. Yet the causes of modern slavery can be overcome, as these initiatives show. We need to bring scale and focus to these great projects, learn from their expertise and help them to grow. Thanks to the experience in their communities of organizations like SAVE, which is bringing educational opportunities to migrant children, and Freeset, which creates decent work for women, there are now effective advisers and consultants able to deliver training to factories that urgently need to design new systems in order to pay a living wage.

India's 'green factory'

The Sree Santhosh Garment Manufactory Company in Tirupur, India, undertakes spinning, knitting, dyeing, printing, embroidery and tailoring. Since the inception of what it proudly calls its 'green factory', it has won countless environmental prizes and operates 'vertical integration', meaning it is in control and has oversight of its entire supply chain. Its largest customer and a strategic partner is Continental Clothing Co. from the UK. Vinoth Kumar (pictured with me in his factory) is Sree Santhosh's Executive Director.

Infographic by Margaux David for Continental Clothing

'My father started this company in 1986 with 10 to 12 sewing machines; every day was hard work! Today we have a large factory that is vertically integrated from the spinning mill to the garment making. This is a 'green factory' – the first garment factory in India to be LEED platinum certified. We are 60-per-cent solar powered, and 90 per cent of the light we use inside the factory is natural light – we designed the factory that way. We also have an eco-friendly humidifying air-conditioning system. All the materials used to build the factory are recycled from brick, glass, scrap metal and cement.

'By building the first truly environmentally friendly factory in India, we are trendsetters. Few people knew what a green textile factory meant and a lot of people have been talking about us in the papers and textile magazines. 'I want everybody to build a factory like this! We want to work in a sustainable way through the triple formula of re-use, reduce and recycle – what we take from the earth we have to give back.

'The Fair Wear Foundation comes twice a year to do routine checks in the factory – to check the earnings and treatment of our workers and the meetings and processes. This process is facilitated and informed by a local NGO called SAVE that specializes in labour rights. There are suggestion boxes and also a telephone number on the notice boards that workers can call if they have any complaints or problems; they can also contact the Fair Wear Foundation or Continental Clothing Co. directly.

'We have two human resources managers and four assistants. The team is strong and sorts out problems immediately. Larger issues are discussed with management. There is a strong and effective workers' committee. The introduction of the FAIR SHARE scheme, which was championed by Continental Clothing Co., has helped our business a lot. Productivity is up and absenteeism is down. Workers used to take seven or eight days' [unauthorized] leave per month; now it is just two or three.

sreesanthosh.com

Miki Alcalde

FAIR SHARE for fair pay

The wholesale company Continental Clothing adopted the following definition of the living wage: 'A living wage should be earned in a standard working week (no more than 48 hours) and allow a garment worker to be able to buy food for herself and her family, pay the rent, pay for healthcare, clothing, transportation and education, and have a small amount of savings for when something unexpected happens.'

The Sree Santhosh Garment Manufactory Company is now working with Continental Clothing to pilot FAIR SHARE T-shirts, a pioneering brand that strives to pay workers a living wage.

Mariusz Stochaj is Head of Product and Sustainability at Continental Clothing. He has worked with the workers' committee, the factory management and local NGOs to calculate a living-wage benchmark for this area of Tirupur, where the factory workers live. (For more on the difference between a living wage and minimum wage, see page 44).

In its pilot phase, the FAIR SHARE project determined the monthly financial requirements of a family of four. It calculated that, rather than the government minimum wage of 285 rupees ($4.18) per eight-hour shift, the lowest-paid workers should receive 466 rupees ($6.83) in order to earn a living wage. This equates to 14,048 rupees ($200) per month before deductions.

Under Mariusz's straightforward scheme, a premium is added to the garment price as a separate cost item and passed directly to workers through their monthly wage packet. The premium is equivalent to about 13 US cents being added to the retail price of a T-shirt and 69 cents to a hoody.

The project has been running since 1 January 2016. Since then, the FAIR SHARE range has made up 10 per cent of the factory's output, with the additional revenues being divided equally among all of the factory's workers. At the moment, the workers are still falling a long way short of earning the living wage, but if consumers embrace the idea that a small increase in the price of clothing can have a direct, positive effect on workers' salaries, the factory could increase wages further, lifting all employees to the living wage. I met up with Mariusz to find out more.

How difficult is it to aim to pay a living wage, and how does it work in practice?
Most brands ask four or five factories for quotes before they decide where to place an order. In this way, they are driving down prices and creating a race to the bottom. Everyone is running on very tight margins and brands know that they can't put demands on factories to improve conditions and pay workers better, so they just say nothing. Someone needs to break this cycle and pay more.

So in the case of FAIR SHARE, who is paying for the living wage?
As a brand we are ring-fencing the FAIR SHARE premium rather than putting it through our normal price calculation that would multiply this, making the product very expensive. We also encourage our retailers to avoid marking up the labour cost increase.

Garment workers benefit from the FAIR SHARE premium that helps bring them closer to a living wage.

Safia Minney

We need to see how consumers react to the idea of paying a FAIR SHARE and how it could be increased. It would also help if regulations were in place in other factories so Continental Clothing was competing on a level playing field.

When will you be able to pay everyone a living wage?

The lowest-paid workers in the factory currently earn about 300 rupees [$4.40] per day. However, the benchmark we set for the living wage is 466 rupees [$6.83], so there is 170-rupee shortfall. At the moment they are only getting a 25-rupee [36-cent] premium extra per shift. It could take five years to reach the target of living wages.

To understand more fully the issues surrounding living wages, it is important to look at the big picture of the local economy. If everybody gets a pay rise, all local prices for rent and food will simply go up accordingly, so no-one but the landlords and shopkeepers will be any better off. Another question is, do we just pay the premium to the first-tier workers, or share it right the way down the supply chain to the people in the spinning mills, for example? We must ask ourselves what the correct way is to go about things: you need to understand what you are doing in a very informed way.

In your model, price increases are shared by the factory, the brand and the consumer.

Yes, the average profit of fashion brands is 18 per cent; luxury and premium brands make about 35 per cent. The profitability of the companies could be distributed sustainably among the workers to make the company stronger and more successful.

We offer other incentives to our workers, too. For example, we put people on a permanent contract after three months and we have a Provident Fund for workers to draw on for large expenses like weddings, funerals or serious illness. As a result of our initiatives, productivity is up, thanks to much less absenteeism.

fairsharefashion.com
continentalclothing.com

Safia Minney

Village women in Thanapara Swallows benefit from Fair Trade livelihoods close to their homes, so they are able to look after their families too.

A bold vision in Bangladesh

"We know that education is the key to helping children escape from poverty and have the best start in life. That's why we started a school here at Swallows, alongside our Fair Trade textile business."

Raihan Ali, Executive Director, Swallows, Thanapara, Bangladesh

Raihan Ali is the Executive Director of Swallows Development Society in Thanapara, the village in Bangladesh where he was born. In 1971, when he was 14, the village was devastated by the Pakistan army during the War of Independence. Thanks to his small build, Raihan's life was spared when the other menfolk in his community were murdered. He went on to lead his family and his community.

The grieving families came up with a bold vision: to create jobs for the daughters and widows who had no choice but to rebuild the community without fathers, sons, husbands, uncles and grandfathers. Since then, Raihan, his wife Guinea (they met as development workers) and their team have worked tirelessly throughout the region, helping over 3,000 families to find ways to escape the poverty trap. At Swallows today there is a thriving Fair Trade handicraft centre which employs 250 women, bringing economic prosperity to the area. As Raihan says: 'Today it is as relevant as ever to provide jobs and good incomes for women in rural areas, as this helps keep families together and the children educated and nurtured.'

Donations and profits from the Fair Trade project have helped to fund the Swallows school, which has 260 pupils between the ages of 5 and 12. Because of its excellent reputation, Swallows has also been asked to set up 20 informal 'classrooms' in neighbouring villages to help 600 children who had dropped out of school to get back on track and back into mainstream schools.

The school at Swallows takes pride in teaching its students about culture and the arts, while also covering maths, science, languages, IT, environmental education and handicraft training. The lessons benefit not only the children of women who work at the Fair Trade project, but also other low-income children from the surrounding villages. A large proportion of the children who attend the Swallows school go on to further education or find work in areas that matter, such as teaching, nursing and social work.

Even though life isn't easy in the countryside around Swallows, it provides the necessities of healthcare and education, and supports family and community cohesion. Values such as environmental stewardship, religious tolerance and enterprise are put into practice around the school. Children grow food organically in the gardens and tend chickens and goats funded by the local microcredit scheme. Everyone takes pride in learning the local, traditional craft skills practised by their mothers and the other women in the community.

At Swallows there is healthy positivity, open-mindedness, integrity, discipline, respect and creativity, all of which help keep human traffickers out. Swallows also helps keep at bay some of the darker shadows of capitalism – greed, corruption and worker exploitation – as it promotes democracy, dialogue and women's rights.

Craft at the heart of the community

'Traditional craft will always have relevance in the textile and fashion industry,' says Raihan Ali, Executive Director of Swallows in Thanapara, Bangladesh. 'There are 100 million artisans in Asia. They work in small groups in rural areas, making handcraft products. Working with craft through Fair Trade means you can directly support people at the grassroots; these are often the most economically marginalized people. Also, providing decent livelihoods through craft production means they don't have to leave their villages and family to work six hours away.

'Swallows' handcraft production centre is the heart of the community, from which we have other development activities such as healthcare, a school and library, and microcredit. We are the first textile group to get the WFTO "Fair Trade guaranteed" label on our textiles and fashion products.

'I started in 1976. I worked very honestly, but we faced many struggles to build Swallows into the organization it is today. It was a great achievement to have the international recognition of the Fair Trade label – I felt very proud. We have a long-term partnership with [ethical fashion brand] People Tree, and their design team visits us regularly to help us with skills training, new ideas, new patterns and new collaborations.

Over 20 the years, the quality of our hand-woven fabric has improved a lot. We are now able to weave and sew silk fabric into dresses, too. Our hand-embroidery designs are more contemporary but are still hand-worked by over 60 artisans who have grown up doing this traditional work with their mothers and grandmothers. Hand-stitching like this brings together women who are sometimes from very different lives and have faced a lot of hardship. They can draw strength from each other and from the group. It is more than just decent work and pay; it is a real sense of community.

'In Bangladesh, women are treated like second-class citizens socially, economically and legally. They do not have equal inheritance rights, just because they are women. Land is the most precious thing here. At Swallows, women can get legal advice on domestic violence, and become more aware of their rights generally. Having work at Swallows means they don't have to leave the village; this is particularly important because half of our 270 women producers are also the head of the household – their children need them close by.

'Like a handmade textile, every thread of our lives supports and interweaves with the others.'

thanaswallows.weebly.com

Safia Minney

Miki Alcalde

Safia Minney

Safia Minney

Creating value through craft

Through my work with trade unions over the past 20 years and my interviews with hundreds of factory-based garment workers, it has become clear to me that what workers want above all else is a decent livelihood in their own village, so that they can stay with their families. Yet conditions and work opportunities in rural areas are so bad that many are forced to move to the cities, working in a large factory and living in a slum. As Latifa told us in Chapter 3, 'I came to Dhaka over 20 years ago. I rarely see my 14-year-old son, who lives with my mother in the village.'

Craft or artisanal activity is the second-largest employer in the developing world, after agriculture, meaning it actually employs more people than fast fashion. However, the hardship that the craft and artisanal communities operate under is rarely recognized, and the sector urgently needs investment. Artisan enterprise puts food on the table, increases local incomes, preserves cultures, revives and promotes innovation and the evolution of traditional skills, and provides employment for hundreds of thousands of individuals around the world, particularly women. Artisans use their hands to create value by making beautiful textiles and other products while earning a living in rural areas. Imagine the benefits to local communities if this sector was invested in properly and given the tax incentives for research and development that pharmaceuticals or technology companies enjoy.

The Fair Trade and social-innovation movements have long lobbied for an approach that would develop new thinking in finance, from microcredit to working capital, to help Fair Trade suppliers in rural areas provide decent and regular work to the poor. Clearly there needs to be widespread change, a move away from policies that favour the rich to those that favour economically marginalized and vulnerable communities. Artisans work in isolated environments, often without business skills, market access or the finance needed for infrastructure to boost production and sales.

Harnessing artisanal power

The Alliance for Artisan Enterprise puts it like this: 'Organizing and harnessing the power of this sector to increase sales and efficiency has the potential to create jobs, increase incomes and foster sustainable community development. Investing in artisans also preserves unique cultural traditions that in many places are at risk of being replaced by lower-quality, machine-made products.

'With appropriate support, the artisan sector provides an opportunity to transform the international economic landscape. Better integrating artisans into global commerce will increase the incomes and standard of living of many individuals and their families in the developing world.'

allianceforartisanenterprise.org

Safia Minney

Miki Alcaide

 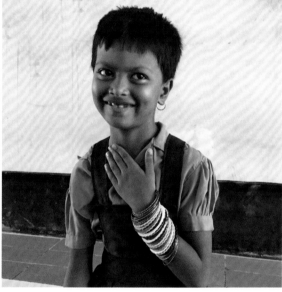

Hova, Gini, Alu and Parveen are growing up at Swallows (see page 108), where their mothers are employed creating handmade Fair Trade clothing.

Safia Minney

The girls attend the Swallows school and have their mothers working close by all day – a luxury afforded to far too few families in Bangladesh.

Freedom through education

Preventing child labour and exploitation starts with one-room schools in the villages around the garment factories. Social Awareness and Voluntary Education, known as SAVE, is an NGO working among the textile and garment-making communities around Tirupur, India. Its mission is to stop the illegal use of child labour and the exploitation of vulnerable women, and to promote a decent standard of living.

It does this through education and advocacy programmes in the community, but also through its active role with local businesses, training factory management teams on the rights of workers and encouraging dialogue between all stakeholders.

Aloysius (see page 65) is the founder, secretary and director of SAVE. He has extensive experience in community development and child protection. There are, he says, 50,000 children aged 14 to 18 working in the spinning mills in Tirupur and at least 2,000 who are under 14 years old. In addition, he estimates that there are 5,000 children who are neither in the factory nor in school but are 'just wandering around'. These children are often to be found rag picking.

'The parents of the children I work with are illiterate,' Aloysius tells me.

'They migrate from thousands of miles away to find work here. Their children have little chance of an education because they can't speak the local language. Whole families end up working in the garment industry for incredibly low wages.

'Rescuing these children and putting them through education will change the future of India. It is exciting to follow their success; some of them go to college to study engineering or business – they achieve wonderful things.'

Many of Aloysius' stories are positive and inspiring, yet without proper legislation and financial and government support, his impact is limited. He explains that once children are taken from a factory and moved into education, the problems are by no means over. In the long term, families need emotional and financial support to keep the children out of factories: 'We have to work hard with the families and children to motivate them to go to school,' he admits. 'It takes time, energy and money.

'The government needs to take responsibility, to put pressure on third- and fourth-tier-level mills and fabric suppliers, to eradicate child labour and forced and bonded labour. There is a law against it, but it is not implemented effectively. Bribery should not be allowed,' says Aloysius. 'Fashion brands

Mary, co-ordinator at SAVE, talks to members of her teen parliament in Tirupur, India.

Miki Alcalde

are starting to talk about social dialogue, which means negotiation talks and collective bargaining. Children under the age of 15 should not be allowed to work in factories and factory owners who employ them should be prosecuted.'

In 2011, SAVE set up teen parliaments in 36 villages, involving 50,000 children aged 11 to 17. The 'ministers' support other children in knowing and fighting for their rights. Fourteen-year-old Alagav, for example, is the Education Minister. She has to check if the children are going to school regularly and to encourage those who drop out to go back to their studies.

The Health Minister will visit sick children absent from school and encourage their parents to take them to hospital. The Minister of Transport makes sure that the local buses run at the right times to get the children to school, and recently successfully lobbied for a bridge to be built over a new road, so that the community wasn't divided by it.

savengo.org

Classes at SAVE run from 9.30am to 4.30pm. The children, who are all from migrant families, are taught in Tamil, the local language, so that after about 18 months they are fluent enough to enter the mainstream government school.

No To Child Labour
Absent
Yes To Child Education
for all.

Miki Alcalde

Miki Alcalde

Freeset

A 'freedom business'

"Freeset is about empowering women to choose freedom from sex-trafficking. They get a fair wage, a pension plan, health insurance and a range of support services. The transformation is amazing. The women, now full of hope, become seamstresses, screen printers, community workers, weavers and managers. In their words, 'Now we can hold our heads up high'."

Kerry Hilton, Co-founder, Freeset, India

Since 2001, Freeset Bags & Apparel has been offering opportunities in a Fair Trade workplace to women trapped in sex work. The company is located in Sonagachi, the largest, most infamous red-light district in Kolkata, India. Within a few square miles, more than 10,000 women stand 'in line' selling their bodies to the thousands of men who visit each day.

Many are trafficked from Bangladesh, Nepal and rural India. For others, poverty has left them with no other choice: the cries of their hungry children drive them to earn money in any way they can.

Freeset, which calls itself a 'freedom business', exists solely to provide employment, dignity and freedom to these women. It produces organic cotton bags and T-shirts for the export market.

I travelled with social worker Mina (whom we met on page 60) and Kerry Hilton, co-founder of Freeset, to one of its rural factories, where we meet Manufa (pictured left), a 20-year-old mother of two. She has worked at Freeset Fabrics in Murshidabad for almost two years.

We arrive to discover that Manufa has prepared lunch for us. After five hours on the road, this is a welcome surprise. As we eat, her children and her proud father sit around us, chatting. Sunshine falls across half of the room, adding to the drama of the elegant, smooth curves of the light-beige handmade mud walls. I follow the clay steps up to the top room, which has just a simple mattress with a mosquito net hanging from the low ceiling. These traditional Bengal homes are perfect for the hot, humid weather. The thick walls keep it cool inside. Then I sit with Manufa to ask her more about her work.

Miki Alcalde

The young girl standing in this photograph is Kirtana. Like Manufa, she grew up in Murshidabad. When her marriage failed after only two years, she was sent to Kolkata by her family to work in the sex trade. Mina (seated cross legged on the floor) helped Kirtana to understand the reality of her situation so she could make her own decision to travel back with us to Murshidabad. We wanted to talk to her parents and get their permission for her to start a new life working at Freeset. We succeeded, and this picture shows Kerry (middle) and Mina arranging the paperwork that Kirtana needed for her future freedom. Three weeks later, Kirtana started working at Freeset as a tailor; her family have since moved to Kolkata to be with her.

Why was Freeset Fabrics started?

To help poor people like me get good work, so we have enough to eat and can send our children to school. Thanks to my work at Freeset, life is much easier for me and my family. People are saying that if they could get a job at Freeset Fabrics they would be really happy.

What other employment opportunities are there for women in these villages?

There is no work for women, only for the men who can go and work in the rice fields, sowing and harvesting. Women can only stay at home: that's why most of the people face terrible financial hardship. The only option for women is to make *bidis* [Indian hand-rolled cigarettes].

Did poverty make you an easy target for traffickers?

I was in such a bad way; after my husband abandoned me I was at my mother's home and a man came from Kolkata and said: 'There is good work for you in Kolkata – you need to go.' I said, 'I'd rather die than go to Kolkata to work.' I was thinking I would take poison and die, but then I worried about what would happen to my children. I imagined that I would give the poison to them first, and then take it myself and end all our lives. I felt so very desperate.

Then one day my sister went to fetch water from the well and met Mina (see page 60) on the road. My sister brought Mina home and she asked me if I would like to work. 'Yes,' I said, 'I want to work!' At that time, my father was working in Mumbai. I called him and he said, 'if you think it will be OK, then do it.' My husband said to me that if I went to work he would break my leg. I said, 'I will see who will break my leg... I will go to work. I don't have enough food to eat or clothes to wear, and I am in so much pain, and no-one is here to help me. If I want to work to survive – what is your problem?'

After starting work at Freeset I received my wages; I came home and my mother and father were very happy. Now in my family we have no problems. I can provide food, clothes and education for my daughters. If they ask, 'Mother, I need that' – I can give it to them.

Have you heard of cases of human trafficking in the villages?

There is one village, next to my uncle's village, called Sondheyjot. One girl was in a terrible state, like I was: she had nothing to eat as there was no work. A man said to her, 'I will give you a job – come, I will take you and give you a good job.' I don't know which village he took her to and sold her. If there is an incident happening in one village, all the other villages come to know about it.

Tell me about the girls who arrive at Freeset from the sex trade.

When girls return from this terrible exploitation, we warmly welcome and accept them. We are ready and waiting to recruit and accept them. We will give them training and a job!

freesetglobal.com
freesetbags.co.uk
freesetusa.com

Manufa and family in Murshidabad, India. Freeset helped her stay with her family and avoid being trafficked into the sex trade in Kolkata, five hours' drive away.

Miki Alcalde

Transparency in the supply chain: how technology can help

It took just 90 seconds for the Rana Plaza building complex in Dhaka to collapse, killing 1,134 garment workers and injuring 2,500 more. So why did it take weeks for some brands to even realize that their clothing was being manufactured there?

Fashion supply chains are complex and murky, characterized by unauthorized subcontracting that involves companies working across many countries. These supply chains have many layers, from procuring fibre and producing fabric, through manufacture and embellishment. Many brands simply don't know where their clothing is being made beyond the first tier, which is garment tailoring. This is a massive problem, because the lack of information makes it impossible for brands to ensure that the human rights of workers and environmental laws are protected in the factories.

Britain's Modern Slavery Act sets an ambitious agenda for transparency, traceability and governance in supply chains, and increasing connectivity between the different stakeholders is vital to its success.

One way we can achieve this is through the application of digital solutions. Information and communications technology (ICT) is already transforming the way we live and work and could have a transformational effect, helping to deliver the new standards of transparency and sustainability that consumers are increasingly demanding. Brands can benefit from

this technology to help them understand their supply chains and change their operations. 'Green wash' is beginning to fall away thanks to pioneering new initiatives that use technology to check and improve workers' rights and safety.

The fashion business is changing. 'Business as usual' will not be enough if we are to deliver the triple bottom line which puts people, planet and profit at the heart of good, sustainable business.

Game-changing technology

Thanks to pioneers such as LaborVoices and LaborLink, technology is now playing a powerful and effective role in providing a meaningful channel for workers to communicate information and data safely and anonymously. Both use SMS technology to connect workers to local support services, such as healthcare and trade unions, as well as aggregating data on employees' working conditions. It is exciting to see the workers themselves becoming the trusted source of information about the working and living conditions they face.

Inspired by this enormous potential, I chatted with a handful of tech start-ups in London about how they think their work can be applied to the question of transparency in the supply chain.

laborvoices.com
goodworldsolutions.org

Safia Minney

By 2020, 90 per cent of the world's population will be covered by mobile broadband networks. I have seen the extent of this first hand, walking through the streets of Dhaka and Phnom Penh, where the price of a smartphone has fallen from $100 to $30. This scale brings unprecedented opportunity to address the exploitation in global supply chains by delivering innovative approaches to connect the unconnected people , even in the most remote and challenging areas.

Once the privilege of the few, falling prices of mobile phones now make them accessible to Bangladesh garment workers, who use them to talk to their families, check for key information and manage their finances.

Miki Alcalde

129

On Our Radar
Be heard

On Our Radar is a small team of journalists, digital storytellers and development workers who are excited about the power of citizen-led information to spark change and inform action. They connect the unconnected, even in the most remote and challenging areas, by creating citizen reporters through mobile technology.

Co-founder and CEO Libby Powell says they have developed software and hardware to promote communication where infrastructure is undeveloped or unreliable. Their network of citizen reporters spans five countries in three continents and reporters send messages to a local telephone number for the price of a standard text. Meanwhile, the editorial team in London sorts, processes and replies to incoming messages through an online dashboard, and shares them directly through social-media accounts.

How does On Our Radar contribute to transparency in garment supply chains?
We specialize in supporting communities that face barriers to engaging in public and digital dialogue. These can be social or economic barriers to sharing information freely, which can hinder transparency and accountability.

When community insight is harnessed, innovation is more likely and solutions are more sustainable. Public audiences and policymakers across the world are more likely to act if they can empathize with the workers.

Why is grassroots storytelling important to the job of eradicating modern-day slavery?
Every human deserves the right to speak up on the matters that affect their lives. Voices from communities can improve industry by offering insight and solutions that are not always obvious to decision-makers. Workers are experts in their own working environments but are rarely consulted.

Statistics reveal a concerning trend, but stories give the human context, which can be the additional fuel needed to nudge people from concern towards action. Stories can rebalance perceptions around data which might be confusing a local situation – for example, the presence of children on a factory floor may be confirmed by a head count and may lead to concerns around child labour, but gathering reports from mothers may reveal that children are joining them due to a lack of childcare and that their presence is tolerated rather than mandated.

What are the biggest barriers to giving people a voice?
New technology has given rise to more mechanisms for workers to communicate their needs and perspectives, using channels that go beyond the traditional route of focus groups and community interviews. SMS short codes and free-phone numbers used in factories or communities offer a route for workers to submit real-time concerns via basic mobile handsets.

But these channels can fail to address and override the social and economic barriers that prevent certain groups from raising their voices. As a result, we often end up hearing from more vocal, less vulnerable people. Women, people with disabilities, elders and children, those with poor literacy, and those living in the more remote or impoverished environments are less likely to use the channels offered without additional support.

Social and self-censorship are also powerful barriers to sharing information: if you have grown up within a culture that rewards subservience and condemns freedom of speech then the arrival of a mobile reporting channel is not going to undo those cultural norms.

onourradar.org

Knowlabel
Be conscious

Knowlabel is a digital label that shows the impact of what you are wearing on people and the planet. Fashion retailers and brands pay to use Knowlabel's solution to show consumers the story behind their products and directly link investment in their supply chains to sales. When you are in store, you just tap the Knowlabel digital label with your phone. Users can discover the story behind products, including impact on people and the planet and how to care for clothing in the most environmentally friendly way.

Marianne Hughes, the founder of this new and innovative start-up, explains that technology can help make the discovery of the stories behind your clothing exciting.

'Consumers lack access to information,' she says. 'Our research on social labelling with 200 consumers in Britain led us to discover a lack of trust, understanding and availability of the information on our clothes. We have worked with Corporate Social Responsibility [CSR] teams and discovered their challenges, for example around measuring the impact of their activities to support the business case. Knowlabel links CSR to sales.

'Digital labelling unites the themes of sustainability and the "internet of things". Digital labelling not only brings together the online and offline communication channels for a brand, it gives them and others along the supply chain a voice to share with the consumer. There is an increasing amount of information out there, and Knowlabel can help put that into a language and format which we can all understand. This mission to eradicate modern slavery and save our planet is huge and urgent, and technology recognized by consumers and large retailers can achieve change at the pace needed.'

Marianne is convinced that consumers are interested in the story behind the products they buy.

'The typical argument that "consumers don't care" is unfair,' she argues. 'I don't believe consumers currently have the option to care, since they don't have access to information on which to base their decisions. Knowlabel allows us to gather data around consumer engagement with sustainability to understand the relationship between consumer interest and purchase.

'I started out as a fast-fashion addict, and I know that my own journey to discover more about the story behind my clothes has really changed what I wear. If I can take others on that journey, I know we will change behaviour; we're humans, not consumers, after all! Instead of calling you a consumer, we encourage you to #beknowlabel, which means to understand your individual and collective impact on people and the planet.'

knowlabel.org

what3words
Be seen

"Without an address, you live outside the law; you might as well not exist."

Hernando de Soto, development economist

The benefits what3words can bring to auditing and improving factory conditions are clear. Garment factories are large, sprawling, hazardous complexes. If workers, or anyone else inside a factory, photograph a locked fire exit, hazardous cabling, empty water tank or any other non-compliance, the site can be exactly located to a three-metre square. This makes it almost impossible for the factory owner to be vague about acknowledging the danger or negligent in fixing it. This photographic, location-specific evidence can also be sent to labour unions who could monitor factory improvements and raise the alarm if they didn't get done.

what3words is a mobile mapping app that gives a unique combination of just three words to identify a three metre by three metre square anywhere on the planet. There are 57 trillion such squares, each with a unique three-word address.

Not having a recognized address is frustrating and costly even in the rich world; in the developing world it can be life-threatening for individuals and limit the country's growth. A three-word address provides a way for anyone to talk about where they live. For some people, it will be the first time they can register themselves for health, financial or government services. An address makes people visible to the state, and allows them to join the formal economy and exercise their rights. In developing countries, an address means that a water point can be monitored and fixed, humanitarian aid can be requested, microfinance can be scaled up, local businesses can thrive, and hospitals and schools can be found. And as Clare Jones, what3words' Global Partnerships Director, explains:

'It also means much better data collection and monitoring and evaluation for NGOs, as they have accurate location data for clients. With more accurate data, supply chains can become more transparent and service delivery can be improved. No-one who needs support cannot be found, whether they live in a slum, a favela or simply a remote, rural region.'

I went to meet chief marketing officer Giles Rhys Jones, to talk about the possibilities of this technology when applied to the garment supply chain.

'There are about four billion people who don't have an address,' Giles told me by way of background. 'If you don't have an address, you are invisible. To get onto the social and economic development ladder, there are three barriers you need to overcome: being unconnected, being unbanked, being unaddressed. The first two are being solved with mobile phones and mobile banking; what3words solves the third.'

I decide to try out what3words on my next factory visit. Needless to say, it is impossible for me to get inside a typical, non-compliant factory with a camera. However, I am able to try out the principle at Fair Trade group TARA Projects in Delhi, India, where they do have good conditions for workers. What if what3words could be used to deliver picture evidence of unsafe conditions and non-compliance in factories around the world?

what3words.com

prefer.assurance.cable

rezoning.rapid.warblers

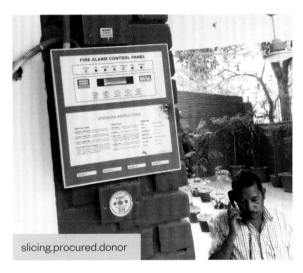

slicing.procured.donor

portfolio.parrot.revert

basher.grad.primary

reboot.unicorn.rinse

Miki Alcalde

Provenance
Be transparent

"Provenance has the potential to aid millions of people around the world to make more sustainable choices about the things they buy – not only end customers, but customers all the way along supply chains."

Jessi Baker, founder, Provenance

The aim of Provenance is to build trust in brands and products by recording and tracking the place of origin (or ownership) of a product in a public, transparent and secure system.

To do this, Provenance uses blockchain technology, which provides a shared database that is transparent and tamper-proof, thereby creating a mark of trust that spans supply chains from source to consumer. As well as authenticity, blockchain provides a concrete way of proving something is sourced in a sustainable manner, and that no slavery, exploitation or other poor practices were involved. Jessi Baker, founder and CEO, explains more.

What motivated you to start Provenance?
A personal frustration with how little we know about the things we buy. There are horrors in supply chains, but also amazing stories. I was frustrated that I couldn't easily and confidently find the products with a positive social impact and avoid supporting the tragedies with my wallet. Provenance is a company I have been dreaming up since 2006. But it isn't just a company, it's really the start of a social movement powered by technology.

Why is blockchain a good tool to use?
Today, supply-chain information is stored in centralized databases, meaning that key data sits in silos. Nobody has access to this information apart from the company who owns the data and whoever they choose to share it with.

Storing key supply-chain data in a decentralized database which is open, secure and inherently auditable is radically different from the status quo. We are able to store verified information without gaining a monopoly on data.

As an open, incorruptible data system, the blockchain empowers every actor in the supply chain, fostering greater equality all along the chain. Beyond this, it enables numerous data systems to connect and communicate in the same language – allowing data to flow seamlessly from producer through to the consumer.

The Modern Slavery Act has made it imperative for business to understand how and where their products are made, but why do you think consumers are interested in the provenance of the things they buy?
In recent years there have been terrible scandals in the food and fashion industries. Unfortunately, these aren't isolated incidents. They have exposed a complex web of untruths, inequality and the reality that opaque supply chains are devastating environments and livelihoods around the world. With the internet and rise of social media, information is shared more easily than ever before. It has become harder and harder to remain ignorant to the lack of equality in global supply chains.

As a result, we're finding that there is a new type of digitally savvy consumer who is demanding more information about the food and goods they buy. People want assurance that the things they are purchasing have not caused harm to the environment and societies from which they originated.

provenance.org

Segura

Be responsible

Today's supply chains are longer and more geographically dispersed than ever. Brands have to understand these complexities if they are going to have any chance of addressing modern slavery. Yet most brands only have real oversight of their first-tier suppliers, and this lack of visibility causes many problems, not least unauthorized subcontracting with its inherent issues of hidden slavery in the workforce.

Segura is a technology platform that addresses this problem through end-to-end mapping of global supply chains and confirming suppliers' compliance. The aim is to give brands a level of transparency that will help mitigate the risk of modern slavery and secure ethically responsible business.

I came across Segura through its sponsorship of the Unchosen Modern Slavery Short Film Competition. Unchosen (unchosen.org.uk) is a UK charity that uses short films and animations to reveal the human stories behind trafficking, forced labour, sexual exploitation and domestic servitude in the UK.

I meet up with Peter Needle, CEO and co-founder of Segura, and ask him why he thinks it is important for brands to know their supply chains, beyond commercial and legislative incentives.

'I think there is an increasing desire from consumers for authentic products,' he replies. 'Businesses exist to make money, so looking after the commercial side is paramount. Historically, I have seen a desire from businesses to become ethical, but never a willingness to pay for it. That is changing. We have proven beyond doubt that the ethical choice is the most profitable choice, and brands are catching on in ever increasing numbers.'

Why do you think consumers care about where their clothes have been made?

My personal view is that, as a society, we have moved beyond the materialism of post-modernism. The up-and-coming generation values authenticity and integrity more highly and want to see that in the products they buy. When I was a teenager I can't say I ever thought about how my clothes were made. It's almost impossible to ignore these days.

What do you hope will be the next steps for technology in supply chains?

You can't influence what you can't measure. Technology has a big role to play. Most brands know little of what's going on in their supply chains beyond the first tier. This means components such as branded labels and hangers could be being made in factories with children or slaves. Currently, brands are spending fortunes auditing their factories to death. If they have no system to ensure the factories they audit are the ones that ultimately make their products, they are wasting their money. Compliance software will play an increasing role in supply chains over the next few years.

segura.co.uk

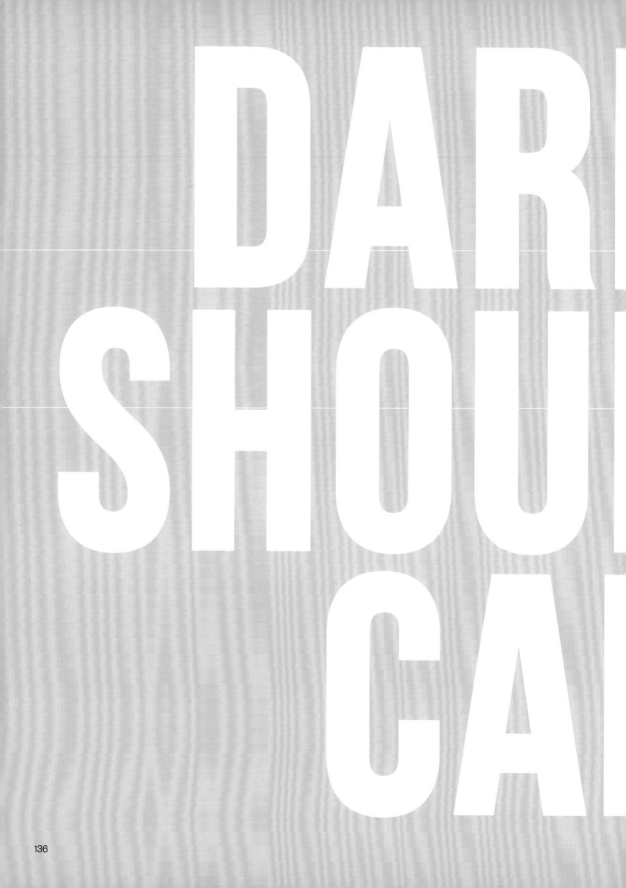

DARK
SHOULD
CAL

You are
the Solution!

YOUR TOOLKIT.

1

Be an activist

Ethical consumerism and beyond.

2

Join the revolution

Six million of us lent our voices to Fashion Revolution week in 2016. Why not get involved this year?

3

Beyond ethical consumerism

We live in a global village – and we all have a role to play in it.

4

Challenge perceptions

Question beauty stereotypes that are unrealistic and unethical.

5

Building better partnerships between buyers and suppliers

Fashion professionals need to take responsibility for tackling modern slavery.

6
Be passionate about fabric

The material used to make your clothes makes a difference.

7
Begin with a T-shirt

Take pride in the provenance of your clothes.

8
Learn from the millennials

Ask questions and dig deeper into the behaviour of your favourite brands.

9
Vote with your wallet

Consumers have power – we just need to use it.

10
What needs to happen now

The low-down on who must do what to eradicate modern slavery in the fashion industry.

11
Resources

Learn more, join campaigns, engage on social media – there are many ways to get involved.

1

Be an activist

I was standing in Oxfam in London's Carnaby Street when I had my first encounter with Fair Trade and ethical business. The charity shop was my favourite lunchtime haunt when I was working in publishing in the late 1980s.

My full-time salary wasn't enough to pay the rent, let alone buy new clothes, and I was juggling two jobs. Surrounded by secondhand garments and unwanted new clothes from Jaeger and other luxury retailers, I stumbled across a book about Third World poverty and the need for Fair Trade. Next to the books section sat bags of Fair Trade coffee and tea: problem and solution, side by side. All I had to do was learn – and then act.

People Tree, the ethical-fashion company I launched in Japan over 25 years ago, started life as a campaigning group called Global Village. Its aim was to inform people about human rights, poverty and environmental issues, and to design Fair Trade products made with respect for people and the planet.

Many years later, when I was collaborating on a Fair Trade capsule collection with *Vogue Japan* and internationally acclaimed designers, using organic-cotton hand-woven fabrics and hand embroidery, journalists used to ask me: 'What's more important to you, selling more Fair Trade products and increasing livelihoods beyond the 5,000 people you already support, or changing the fashion industry with your campaigning work?' But for me, it has always been about both.

From the very first year of People Tree, we ran Saturday-night study meetings with homemade, vegetarian, organic food. We ran stands at festivals and gave talks about Fair Trade.

We joined and led protests and petitions on World Trade Organization and G8 trade issues; we invited politicians, ambassadors, opinion leaders and buyers to our Fair Trade fashion shows and encouraged them to join 'hunger banquets' at the first People Tree shop (at a hunger banquet we would give a third of the guests rice and beans, a third of them a luxury meal,

War on Want

and a third a crust of bread and a glass of water, to give them a first-hand experience of inequality).

As I visited communities in the developing world, I learnt about the causes of and solutions to global poverty. I told the stories of those I had met, and found that Fair Trade captured the imagination of most of the people I spoke to. Telling these stories reflected the integrity of the partnership and trust we built with our producer partners and together we pioneered sustainable best practice.

I started to bring Fair Trade leaders from India, Bangladesh, Nepal and Kenya over to Britain to give talks and meet journalists, and I arranged for opinion leaders, journalists and designers to travel with me to the developing world to see for themselves the difference that Fair Trade and a sustainable design-led approach made to economically marginalized communities.

World Fair Trade Day, which I initiated in 2001, has become the focal point for the Fair Trade movement to celebrate, in myriad culturally diverse ways, its achievements and to promote its aims.

As consumers, we have the power to take a stand against our dysfunctional capitalist system, to make purchasing choices that reflect who we are and how we want the world to be. Things have moved on since the early days of the Fair Trade movement and pioneers such as the Body Shop. I was swept up in the first wave of ethical consumerism and activism on that inauspicious day in Oxfam over 30 years ago. Today, we can all be part of the second wave, which is being driven by social media and digital innovation, to ensure transparency in supply chains and demand an end to modern slavery and worker exploitation. There is also an important place for protests and writing to MPs and brands.

This chapter provides many of the tools you need to make a difference, while also highlighting some innovative projects that you can support and learn from as you continue on your own ethical journey.

🐦 @SafiaMinney
📷 @safia_minney
safia-minney.com

2

Join the revolution

24 April is Fashion Revolution Day. Founded in 2013 by fashion designers Carry Somers and Orsola de Castro, it raises awareness of the true cost of fashion and shows the world that change is possible. It's easy to get involved – online, on social media and in person. I went to meet Sarah Ditty, Head of Policy at Fashion Revolution, to find out more.

'Four years after the Rana Plaza disaster, Fashion Revolution's 2017 campaign focuses on Money, Fashion, Power. We are asking consumers to think about who is actually getting the profits from what we all wear. People can understand the financial story of what they are buying – that you are voting with your wallet.

'Last year's #whomademyclothes campaign was seen over 150 million times on social media and saw events across 90 countries. We now have hundreds of producers' stories on our website. We aim to educate people more and more about the true story behind the clothes they wear.

'In some ways, the UK is setting the agenda and showing leadership. We have also seen exciting campaigns and events in Italy, Spain and Australia. In Brazil, a team rented a shop on a busy high street and dressed the window with fast-fashion 'bargain sale' deals. When customers went inside, they were lambasted with the reality of sweatshop conditions.

'The shop was dark and oppressive, and they were surrounded by sounds of sewing machines and videos of garment workers. Customers really got a sense of

the reality of the lives of people who are struggling to make the clothes they buy.

'In 2016 we partnered with Ethical Consumer to launch a Transparency Index (nin.tl/FR-index). We want to put pressure on brands to disclose more information about their supply chain, so that civil society, trade unions and journalists can check up on the ethical claims made by companies and dig deeper, making sure that brands are accountable for what they are doing.

'The Index is also educational for consumers, as it helps them to understand what questions they should be asking brands.

'Most people have no idea that slavery still exists in fashion supply chains. A lot of people don't know that the UK's Modern Slavery Act exists; in fact, a lot of companies don't know it exists! We need a government-backed website for businesses to log their supply chain reports, as required by the Act. Ultimately, we need some sort of Ombudsman where people can go to file a complaint against companies that are not fulfilling their obligations.

'Our vision is of a fashion industry that values people, planet, profit and creativity in equal measure. If all of these things were genuinely valued in a moral as well as financial sense, we would have a different world.'

🐦 @Fash_Rev
📘 fashionrevolution.org
📌 fashrevglobal
📷 fash_rev
fashionrevolution.org

3

Beyond ethical consumerism

Clean Clothes Campaign (CCC) has led the way in campaigning in the Global South and North for better conditions for garment workers while pressurizing brands to improve their practice (read more on page 14). I talked to Sam Maher, international co-ordinator of CCC, about what we need to do about ethical consumption.

'It's not about consumers being able to choose; it's about consumers being able to act. People feel powerless to act beyond where they can spend their money. In many neighbourhoods, there's nowhere to buy ethical or Fair Trade products; there's just a supermarket. People need to know what to do to get involved. Guilt is a very negative emotion to use to try to promote change; it makes people feel powerless. People should think about how they shop and what they buy.

'We are powerful as a collective movement. The trade-union movement, CCC and others act together as a powerful political force. You might feel that signing a petition is meaningless, but educating yourself, getting involved with debate, raising the issues with MPs, and supporting living-wage movements in your area is very important. Contributing to an overall political movement is critical.

'It may not feel that it's worth turning up for a shop action or leafleting people, but all of these things together are part of the collective movement which involves consumers and workers.

'Workers in the developing world are actively involved. They are not just waiting for us to save them, but we should be uniting with them. This is not just about being a consumer; it is about being an engaged citizen and having a view about the global village that we live in and the part we play in it.'

Clean Clothes Campaign

CCC activists protest in solidarity with Cambodian workers' demand for a monthly wage of $177, December 2015.

@cleanclothes
cleanclothescampaign
cleanclothes.org

4

Challenge perceptions

Billie Scheepers

Mainstream media and fast fashion peddle images of 'ideal' body shapes that are both unrealistic and destructive. One way to move towards a more ethical, caring fashion industry is to question beauty stereotypes and to raise awareness of diversity. Caryn Franklin, fashion commentator and Professor of Diversity in Fashion at Kingston University, has just completed her degree in Applied Psychology. She talks about her fashion activism and offers advice for the ethical consumer.

How have you helped to set the agenda for body diversity?

I have worked in fashion for 35 years and for the last 25 of them I have been challenging the promotion of the 'fashion normative' body (thin, white and young) as too limited for good mental health. I know many young women and, increasingly, young men who are negatively affected by the glamorous images they see so often. Back in the early 1990s, this work involved speaking out in the media and making documentaries. I also felt compelled to challenge racial myopia where I saw it. It was always important to me to have a range of skin tones and origins represented.

We need to demand diversity in front of the lens, but to achieve that we also need diversity behind the lens. That means getting more women and people of colour into influential positions in the fashion industry.

What lessons about creating a fashion industry free of worker exploitation and slavery can we learn from you?

I hope all my audiences understand that they have the power to change things by getting together and using the power of the purse. They can place their money and social-media support behind Fair Trade and ethical brands that are attempting to be transparent and support workers rather than enslave and exploit them. We engage with fashion for fun and self-esteem, but how is it possible to feel good knowing that a garment has been produced in an exploitative way? Psychology tells us that people even take on the qualities of what they wear; it affects the way the brain processes. There are many exciting findings coming through from the London College of Fashion's new Applied Psychology in Fashion course, and this will help progress desire for Fair Trade.

How can consumers buy better on a budget?

Quality clothes that are well made can be found through secondhand stores. Fine tailored garments, knitwear, leather belts or bags, silk blouses – these are all basic building blocks in your wardrobe. Then search online for emerging businesses: Asos market place, for example, supports young designers, many of whom are making small runs in the UK. Or look for designers specializing in upcycled clothing.

Most of all, take pride in your individuality. Stop copying others and be your own unique self. Trends are a tool for magazines and retailers to present fashion in a coherent way, but you don't have to follow. Some of my favourite clothes are things I bought from the bargain bin because they were too 'out there'. Expect to change the shape of garments to fit you better; make temporary changes with safety pins. I'm a big fan of safety pins!

Caryn_Franklin
franklinonfashion.com

5

Building better partnerships between buyers and suppliers

Tamsin Lejeune is the founder of the Ethical Fashion Forum (EFF). The mission of EFF is to support and promote sustainable practices, facilitate collaboration, raise awareness and provide tools and resources needed to reduce poverty, reduce environmental damage, and raise standards in the fashion industry. Tamsin explains why fashion professionals need to take responsibility for tackling modern slavery.

'Awareness needs to increase amongst fashion professionals (and consumers) of the existence of slavery, how it can occur in fashion-industry supply chains, and what they can do about it. Through the EFF resource platform, we offer information, training and shared best practice, in order to support increased awareness.

'I believe that closer partnerships between brands and suppliers will be a driver for change. We operate in a divided industry – with production spread across the world, often thousands of miles from where brands are based. There are cultural and language barriers, there is often a lack of understanding and sometimes lack of trust between buyers, factory owners and workers which leads to opacity. In many cases, buyers don't have the full picture on what is going on in their supply chains, and are not incentivized to find out. Yet when strong partnerships are created, with the different players connecting on a human level and establishing common goals, this

can be transformative. We're building a platform that will facilitate closer partnerships across the fashion supply chain.

'When Naomi Klein's *No Logo* was published in 1999, this, alongside major garment sweatshop exposures, started to catalyse change. A generation of entrepreneurs was inspired to do business differently, and consumer confidence in big business plummeted. But 20 years on, sweatshops and slave labour continue to be widespread.

'I'd like to see the Modern Slavery Act as the beginning of a more regulated approach to fashion production processes. From tax incentives for best practice to penalties for social and environmental bad practice, government and international regulation offers the fastest and most impactful route to change.

'By setting the bar high and proving what can be achieved through exemplary business practices, Fair Trade and social enterprise is already creating the agenda for a better fashion industry. The great opportunity that lies ahead of us is that if we work collaboratively, we can scale this up. I believe that we can make sustainable fashion the norm – rather than the exception to it. It's an exciting goal to get behind.'

🐦 @EthicalFashionF
f ethicalfashionforum
ethicalfashionforum.com

Abury, www.abury.net, photography by Suzana Holtgrave

Bav Tailor, www.bavtailor.com

Mayamiko, www.mayamiko.com

Behno, www.behno.com

6

Be passionate about fabric

The quality of the materials used to make your clothes makes a big difference – not just to you and your skin, but also to the producers, who are paid a living wage and work in decent conditions without exposure to dangerous chemicals
By being more discerning about the clothes you choose to wear, you can help support Fair Trade and ethical fashion. Charlie Ross, founder of Offset Warehouse, has turned her passion for textiles into a thriving sustainable fabric business.

'I am completely obsessed with fabrics! My love affair began with a degree in fashion design. During my Masters at the Royal College of Art I became aware of the terrible social and environmental impact of the textile and fashion industry. Until then, it had never crossed my mind that big brands could actively be exploiting workers or dumping hazardous chemicals into our rivers, soil and air in order to squeeze out every last penny of profit.

'I decided I would only use ethically produced fabrics in my work, which is when my challenge began. Sourcing good textiles without compromising my ethics was a nightmare! The only eco-friendly fabrics I could find were either incredibly expensive or had huge minimum order quantities. So, after I graduated, I made it my mission to solve this problem – and began Offset Warehouse.

'Most mass-market fabrics are produced by untrained, underpaid, overworked staff in unsafe surroundings. Many textiles require highly toxic chemicals to produce them, and these are often handled by workers without the proper safety equipment. The philosophy of Offset Warehouse is to ensure that the people who make our fabrics are safe and treated properly. All our suppliers are paid fairly and operate in surroundings that do not endanger their health.

'We also work with very small communities, who weave outside their houses and choose their own hours. They set their own prices and their manufacturing timelines, and we never, ever pressure them to reduce their prices. Giving the dyers and weavers regular, reliable work that they control brings their communities financial stability and sustainability and, with it, the ability to plan for their families' futures.

'I pride myself in seeking out the most beautiful, handcrafted and fairly sourced fabrics, trims and threads from across the globe and selling them in quantities, and at prices, which make them accessible to everyone.'

🐦 @OffsetWarehouse
offsetwarehouse.com

Make a zero-waste dress

Did you know that on average, 15 per cent of fabric is wasted every time a garment is made? One way to eliminate this is to design clothes that are 'zero waste', where the sewing pattern uses all the fabric and nothing is thrown away. Offset Warehouse has put together a simple zero-waste dress pattern so you can try it for yourself.

1 Head to **offsetwarehouse.com**
and order your ethical fabric. We'd be delighted to help you with your choice, and also advise on how much you need, so please get in touch: info@offsetwarehouse.com.

2 **Download detailed instructions here for free:**
offsetwarehouse.com/resources/ slave-to-fashion.html

3 As well as your fabric you'll need a sewing machine, paper to draw your pattern onto, a pencil or pen, pins, a needle, thread, paper scissors, fabric scissors, fabric chalk, an iron and a long ruler.

4 Following the instructions, lay out your pattern in the most fabric-efficient way.

5 Cut out the pattern pieces using sharp dressmaking scissors.

6 Follow the simple sewing instructions and, hey presto, you will have made your own zero-waste garment!

7 Sewing time is between 4 and 12 hours, depending on your level of experience.

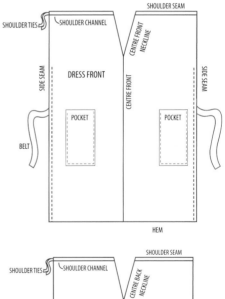

Model: Sonny, Milk Management; Hair & Make-up: Louise Dartford; Stylist: Claire Ginzler; Photographer: charneymagri.com retoutcherbox.co.uk; Shoes: Bourgeois Bohème, Accessories: Louisewade@jewellery.

Azul Aramburu is a Spanish fashion and print designer. Having worked for high-fashion labels such as Jonathan Saunders and Emilio de la Morena, she is currently the designer of Sister Jane. Azul refuses to believe that fashion cannot be sustainable. By designing this jumpsuit with a hand-woven Fair Trade fabric from Swallows (available through Offset Warehouse), she wanted to demonstrate that ethical fashion can be as stylish and as appealing as fast fashion.

azularamburu/
azularamburu.studio/

Model : TESS Management & Ella Hope Merryweather; Photographer : James Champion

Justine Tabak jumped at the opportunity of working with an ethical, Fair Trade fabric from Artisan Hut. 'I loved the subtle patterns and texture of the jacquard. The fashion industry has become too globalized, churning out endless copies of catwalk looks with very little thought for true individuality. So my message would be: slow down, consider your decisions and start to celebrate creative individuality for the greater good.'

justine_tabak/
justinetabak.co.uk
artisanhutbd.com

7

Begin with a T-shirt

'There is a big difference between "apparel" (the clothes we wear to cover up or keep warm), and "fashion",' says designer Matthew Gordon. 'Fashion is an art, not a necessity; it's a way to express yourself and your place in the world. That's why it's important to show respect for all the people involved in making it. If you want to say you're into fashion, you have to take care about and pride in where it was made.

'There is a real market for Fair Trade and organic T-shirts, but the problem is that people make it out to be some sort of charity, which it isn't. Paying people properly is just the right thing to do!

'As far as I can see, marketing a brand around ethical and sustainable messages has never worked. All you need is a good designer, who happens to use ethical and sustainable materials; they just need to know what they're doing. It's not hard to source these materials. FAIR SHARE (see page 104) was an obvious choice for me. I know how badly some garment workers are treated, and I don't want to be responsible for giving them an even harder life.

'Organic cotton feels really nice and lasts much longer than ordinary cotton. I want my customers to know that feeling. They might not know it is organic when they buy it, but they'll experience it over time.

'I work under the name "Boiler Boyz"; it's not a brand because it doesn't really have a fixed style; it's all about being spontaneous. Designs originate from what Lewis [the photographer] and I are thinking about from day to day – as we change, the designs change. Because of this speed we need to do very short runs,

maybe only 20 or 25 pieces. For a quick turn-around, the logistics need to be simple and straightforward. We use just one size and shape of basic T-shirt for each design and buy from and print at one place. We sell everything through social networks. The tiny extra cost of using organic and FAIR SHARE T-shirts is just part of the deal – that's like asking, "What about the extra cost of good design?"

'It's just basic to expect quality, ethics and design when you buy fashion now. They are all equally valued by customers and very possible to achieve; brands that say otherwise are just not creative enough to see the potential.

'My friends and I are not simply interested in making money, we want to make something substantial.

My message to other designers is to think hard about who you want to be and what you want to say, then act accordingly. And to consumers, I would say: "Don't just do the obvious and buy fast, mass-produced fashion. Be an individual: it will make you feel good!"'

:camera: mattgordon0211

photograph - @royalblend_..; model - @antoniaczezowska

8

Learn from the millennials

Consumers born in the last couple of decades of the 20th century love information (they are used to having it at their fingertips) and looking beyond brand names to the values associated with them. Their more engaged way of shopping is something we can all draw inspiration from. Project JUST is an online community committed to changing the way we shop for fashion by reviewing fashion brands for their supply-chain ethics and sustainability, and awarding their Seal of Approval to the top brands in the industry. Co-founder Natalie Grillon shares her insights into a generation of canny consumers.

'A lot of our generation feels like we got taken for a ride [in the recession]: things that were "true" turned out not to be true. We don't trust corporations, we don't trust the banks or the associated system.

'Just to have a brand name isn't enough. You're supposed to talk about what your process is and how your product is made. You're supposed to tell us about the people who make it. We love to meet the people who are behind the brand.

'That's why the degree to which a company is transparent and authentic about how it makes its products resonates with the millennial shopper: we're going to tell you exactly how much money goes into making this product, and our profit margin. We're going to show you who are the people making the clothes; we're going to show you the factory.

'We've seen from the California Transparency Act [see page 24] that many brands say they're in compliance. But there's no evidence to support it because nobody is enforcing it. Shoppers can support brands that support the Transparency Act but people don't have the time or energy to look into compliance. Project JUST has a theory of how consumers change their behaviour. First, they become aware: "This is something I need to pay attention to, just like I paid attention to it with food." Then they say, "OK, I'm going to engage in this issue. I'm going to start to look for clothing that has either a Fair Trade mark or it's a brand a friend has told me about." Finally, they start to shift their practices and their actual behaviour changes.

'I think 50 per cent or more of millennials would shift their behaviour if information was more readily available and if it became cooler to shop ethically. Vintage has become really popular. It's OK to wear secondhand clothes. We need to feed into that trend.

'People want to be part of a group or tribe. If we can offer them opportunities to join communities that reflect their aspirational view of themselves, we can start to change their behaviour. The brands that are successful nowadays are the ones that reflect the kind of person you want to be; ones that are aligned with your values.'

🐦 @Project_JUST
📷 @ProjectJUST
projectjust.com

9

Vote with your wallet

"The California transparency law has been a terrific first step. What we need now is a national business-transparency law with rigorous disclosure and enforcement procedures."

Terry FitzPatrick, Communications Director, Free the Slaves

Rebecca Ballard is a public-interest lawyer and founder of ethical fashion label Maven Women. Though some progress is being made in the US to address modern slavery, consumers should put further pressure on companies by choosing ethical products, she says.

What is the United States doing to prevent slavery in supply chains?

In 2010, the State of California enacted the California Transparency in Supply Chains Act [see page 24], which requires larger companies in California to report on their websites their efforts to eradicate slavery and human trafficking from their supply chain. And in 2016, Congress strengthened this by saying that any goods produced with forced labour (including slave, convict, child or indentured labour) can't be imported into the US. There's a lot of work to be done by US Customs now!

What else should lawmakers do?

Disclosure is good, but it doesn't mandate action. In the same way that we insure safety standards for food and pharmaceuticals, we need to be sure that the clothes and products we use every day are free of slave labour. It wouldn't be hard to require large companies to partner with an NGO, undertake an audit, or receive certification from internationally respected accreditors. We also need a co-ordinated effort across multiple federal government agencies to implement change. One agency can't solve this problem alone.

How can Fair Trade labels compete in the open market?

An uneven playing field has developed with a race to the bottom. I'm a big fan of incentivizing companies with good practices and penalizing those that should do more. No-one should be competing with companies producing goods with slave labour; their goods will always be cheaper. Right now there are no economic benefits for companies that have 'best in class' supply chains, like Fair Trade groups.

Changing US federal law around tariffs could make a huge difference in levelling the playing field. It would be transformative for the federal government to have reduced or eliminated tariffs for ethical companies creating products certified by internationally respected accreditors.

What can consumers do?

Consumers have more power than they realize by voting with their wallets and buying only ethical and sustainable products. It takes a little research, but once customers find a company they like it is easy to sign up for regular news and communications.

Once you get used to buying fewer, higher-quality items, you'll wonder why you ever bought so many low-quality pieces that never really fit!

🐦 @MavenWomen
mavenwomen.com

10

What needs to happen now?

Eradicating modern slavery in the fashion industry has to be a joint effort: governments, law enforcers and consumers all have a responsibility to take action to persuade businesses to be transparent and to change their working practices. Kevin Hyland, the UK's first independent Anti-Slavery Commissioner, explains who should do what, and how.

This is what we need:
- A shift in culture – business leaders need to understand that modern slavery and exploitative working conditions directly affect them and their company. After all, slavery in supply chains is bad business.
- Protection measures for workers – human life is worth more than any profit margin, and a company's greatest assets are the people they employ.
- Improved processes so that transparency of supply chains is achievable and manageable, and clear standards are met and maintained.

Governments must:
- Set an example, ensuring their own suppliers are transparent and slavery free.
- Continue to put pressure on businesses to report what is being done to combat modern slavery(in Britain, under Section 54 of the Modern Slavery Act).
- Work with trade bodies to encourage collective action within sectors; no company can act alone and we need to work together to achieve ambitious targets.
- Empower those in law enforcement to respond to the crime of slavery with efficiency, urgency and excellence.

Law enforcers must:
- Lead on training those in law enforcement well and share training models with other agencies internationally.
- Treat modern slavery as the serious organized crime that it is.
- Boost their efforts and resources to dramatically disrupt criminal networks.

Miki Alcalde

We can make the fashion industry a tool for change and build opportunities to empower women.

Consumers should:

- Question where they shop – we therefore need to increase public awareness of this issue so that people understand the serious organized crime that it is.
- Choose not to shop in certain places – we will eventually see profits plummet, one shopper at a time. Through this, business leaders will wake up and respond to slavery as they should.

Civil society should:

- Continue to create websites that collate TISC [Transparency in the Supply Chain] statements. Since the introduction of the Modern Slavery Act in the UK, many people have called for a central repository of statements. This is not a legal requirement or anticipated to be a function of the state, but a responsibility that lies with civil society. Some organizations have therefore set up their own registry where statements are collated to then be analysed and benchmarked. I am looking into these models to endorse accordingly.

The Independent Anti-Slavery Commission will continue to:

- Work with targeted sectors both domestically and internationally, providing support to companies and increasing awareness/understanding.
- Write to CEOs to inform them of their responsibilities under the Act and provide support where needed.
- Work with other countries to ensure their response to modern slavery is up to standard, predominantly top source countries to UK victims of trafficking, e.g. Vietnam, Nigeria and Romania.
- Work with parliamentarians in selected Commonwealth states to see if and how the Act could be translated and passed through their parliaments. We want the Act to be replicated, but we don't want to make it complicated for businesses that would need to make different statements for different countries.

11

Resources

Pry before you buy

There are many online and digital resources you can use to check how ethical and sustainable your favourite brands are.

Avoid Plugin avoidplugin.com
A browser plugin that screens your browsing activity for products associated with child labour.

Balu getbalu.org
Translates the web into ethical choices for the conscious consumer.

Behind the Barcode baptistworldaid.org.au
Tells you where you can shop ethically.

Ethical Consumer ethicalconsumer.org
A list of ethical brands.

Fairtrade Foundation fairtrade.org.uk
Lists ethical brands – see especially the Fashion Transparency Index compiled in association with Fashion Revolution: nin.tl/FRindex

Good on You goodonyou.org.au
Ethical shopping app.

Not My Style notmystyle.org
An app that tells you how much fashion brands share about how they treat those who make our clothes.

Positive Luxury positiveluxury.com
A list of ethically 'positive' luxury brands.

Slavery Foot Print® slaveryfootprint.org
This app helps you to find out how many slaves work for you.

UK Modern Slavery Act & Registry
business-humanrights.org/en/
uk-modern-slavery-act-registry
A registry of company statements under the UK Modern Slavery Act.

Read more

The Travels of a T-shirt in the Global Economy by Pietra Rivoli

Empire of Cotton – A Global History by Sven Beckett

The Race to the Bottom by Alan Tonelson

Threadbare – Clothes, Sex & Trafficking by Anne Elizabeth Moore

To Die For: Is Fashion Wearing Out the World? by Lucy Siegle

The Promise and Limits of Private Power – Promoting Labour Standards in a Global Economy by Richard M Locke

Naked Fashion – The Sustainable Fashion Revolution by Safia Minney

Fashion & Sustainability – Design for Change by Kate Fletcher & Lynda Grose

Slow Fashion – Aesthetics meets Ethics by Safia Minney

The Song of the Shirt by Jeremy Seabrook

Stitched Up: The Anti-Capitalist Book of Fashion by Tansy E Hoskins

Watch more

The True Cost by Untold Films

Triangle – Remembering the Fire by HBO

Schmatta – Rags to Riches to Rags by HBO

Poverty Inc – Fighting Poverty is Big Business directed by Michael Matheson Miller

US resources

Dhana Inc bthechange.com/directory/dhana-inc/
An award-winning ethical fashion brand for youth.

Modavanti modavanti.com
A great movement towards sustainable fashion.

Le Souk lesouk.co
Online market place for sourcing sustainable fabrics.

Add your voice

Join these campaigning organizations fighting to end modern slavery.

Alliance 8.7 alliance87.org
Our mission is to eradicate forced labour, modern slavery, human trafficking and child labour.

Amnesty International amnesty.org
Standing up for humanity and human rights.

Anti-Slavery International antislavery.org
Works with all stakeholders from a grassroots to an international level to eradicate slavery and its causes from the world.

Clean Clothes Campaign cleanclothes.org
Improving working conditions in the global garment industry.

50 For Freedom Campaign 50forfreedom.org
Making a stand to end modern slavery.

Free the Slaves freetheslaves.net
Liberating slaves and changing the conditions that allow slavery to persist.

International Labour Organization ilo.org
A UN agency bringing together governments, employers and worker representatives to set labour standards promoting decent work for all women and men.

Labour Behind the Label labourbehindthelabel.org
Campaigning for garment workers' rights worldwide.

Unchosen unchosen.org.uk
A unique charity that uses short film and animation to tell people about modern slavery in the UK.

UNICEF unicef.org
Protecting children who are in danger.

Walk Free walkfree.org
Fighting to end modern slavery.

War on Want waronwant.org
Works to achieve a vision of a just world, through its mission to fight against the root causes of poverty and human rights violations, as part of the worldwide movement for global justice.

Engage on social media

There are lots of links to journalists, campaigners, researchers, grassroots organizations and online publications throughout this book; here are some more of my favourites. Follow them, and make your voice heard too!

Amnesty International @amnesty

Copenhagen Fashion Summit @CphFashSummit

Carry Somers @Carrysomers

Clean Clothes @cleanclothes

CottonConnect @Cotton_Connect

Dilys Williams @dilyswilliams

Dress for Our Time @ProfHelenStorey

Ecouterre @Ecouterre

Fashion Takes Action (Canada) @FTAorg

Fashion Revolution @Fash_Rev

Foro de Moda Ética Latinoamérica @ForoModaEtica

International Labour Organization @ilo

just-style.com @juststyle

LabourBehindTheLabel @labourlabel

Lucy Siegle @lucysiegle

Orsola de Castro @orsoladecastro

Oxfam International @Oxfam

Redress Hong Kong @Redress_Asia

Safia Minney @safiaminney

Sustainable Brands @SustainBrands

Tamsin Blanchard @tamsinblanchard

Tansy E Hoskins @TansyHoskins

TriplePundit.com @TriplePundit

True Cost Movie @truecostmovie

War on Want @WarOnWant

charneymagri.com

Bronwyn Seier is a creative thinker and fashion maker from Canada. She is drawn to design for its possibility to create change, and believes that the first step in ensuring brands are held accountable for how they treat the people who make our clothes is for 'consumers to question where their clothing comes from.' The dress in the photo 'aims to create a dialogue with the viewer about the reality of offshore production.'

🄾 bronwyn_seier
bronwynseier.com